Guns Save Lives
True Stories
of Americans
Defending Their Lives
With Firearms

Guns Save Lives
True Stories of Americans Defending Their Lives With Firearms

by Robert A. Waters

**Loompanics Unlimited
Port Townsend, Washington**

Neither the author nor the publisher assumes any responsibility for the use or misuse of information contained in this book. It is sold for entertainment purposes only. Be warned!

Guns Save Lives

True Stories of Americans Defending Their Lives With Firearms

© 2002 by Robert A. Waters

Published by:
Loompanics Unlimited
PO Box 1197
Port Townsend, WA 98368

Loompanics Unlimited is a division of Loompanics Enterprises, Inc.
Phone: 360-385-2230
Fax: 360-385-7785
E-mail: service@loompanics.com
Web site: www.loompanics.com

Cover by Craig Howell

ISBN 1-55950-226-6
Library of Congress Card Catalog Number 2002103440

Contents

Dedication

This book is dedicated to Marilyn. After nearly 30 years of marriage, you're still the best wife and friend a man could have. A special thanks for your support over the last five years as I embarked on a career as a writer. Without your assistance, I would never have gotten one, much less two, books published.

Acknowledgements

Thanks to my brother John, editor, revisionist, and fisherman extraordinaire!

Thanks to Sim and LeAnn for keeping my home life, uh, shall I say, interesting.

I owe a debt of gratitude to my father, John T. Waters, for providing a loving home with traditional values.

My sister Kim and my brother Zack have always been there with support and encouragement. Thanks.

An extra-special thanks to Sean Dodson, Director of Firearms Tactical Institute for helping me with the technical side of firearms. Any mistakes having to do with guns made in the book were my own fault for failure to follow Sean's direction and advice.

Thanks to Richard Stevens, author of *Dial 911 and Die*, and co-author of *Death by "Gun Control,"* for his continued enthusiasm about my book.

Richard Griffith helped with certain interviews, and I appreciate his assistance.

Thanks to Ed Wolfe and Michael Cannon for their continued support and encouragement.

Gia Cosindas, Editor at Loompanics Unlimited, was always informative and cheerful. Thanks.

And Michael Hoy, President of Loompanics Unlimited, deserves a special place in my heart for accepting my book for publication.

I wish to thank all those who consented to interviews from a stranger who called them on the telephone. Interviews about violent confrontations are rarely pleasant, but each individual I talked with made me feel comfortable. They also provided me with newspaper clippings, police reports, court documents, photographs, and, in some cases, their own written descriptions of the events as they unfolded. These people are true American heroes. Because they chose to be armed, they prevented crimes from happening not only to themselves but to many others.

Finally, the support system at the Central Church of Christ cannot be overstated. The Christians there are like family to me, and I appreciate them more than they will ever know. It's sometimes difficult being a Christian in 21st century America, but hasn't it always been? With the help of all my fellow workers at Central, I hope to someday make it home.

Foreword

(This is the transcript of a speech delivered on the Senate floor by Senator Larry Craig, R-Idaho, on June 6, 2000. His explanation of the reasons our Founding Fathers included the Second Amendment in the Bill of Rights should be read and studied in all classrooms in America. Thanks to Senator Craig for allowing it to be reprinted here.)

Mr. President, I appear on the floor to speak about the provision of the Constitution of our country that has been under nearly constant attack for eight years. In fact, we heard on the floor this morning two Senators speak about provisions in law that would alter a constitutional right.

The provision I am talking about is part of our Bill of Rights — the first ten amendments to our Constitution —which protect our most basic rights from being stripped away by an overly zealous government, including rights that all Americans hold dear:

The freedom to worship according to one's own conscience;
The freedom to speak or write whatever we might think;
The freedom to criticize our government;
And, *the freedom to assemble peacefully.*

Among the safeguards of these fundamental rights, we find the Second Amendment. Let me read it clearly: *"A well-regulated Militia, being necessary to the security of a free*

State, the right of the people to keep and bear Arms shall not be infringed."

Some — even of my colleagues — will read what I have just quoted from our Constitution quite differently. They might read, "A well regulated Militia," and stop there and declare that "the right of the people to keep and bear Arms" actually means that it is a right of our Government to keep and bear arms because they associate the militia with the government. Yet under this standard, the Bill of Rights would protect only the right of a government to speak, or the right of a government to criticize itself, if you were taking that same argument and transposing it over [to] the First Amendment. In fact, the Bill of Rights protects the rights of people from being infringed upon by Government — not the other way around.

Of course, we know that our Founding Fathers in their effort to ratify the Constitution could not convince the citizens to accept it until the Bill of Rights was established to assure the citizenry that we are protecting the citizens from Government instead of Government from the citizens.

Others say that the Second Amendment merely protects hunting and sport shooting, that shooting competitions and hunting for food are the only legitimate uses of guns. Therefore, they conclude that the Second Amendment is no impediment to restricting gun use to those purposes.

In fact, the Second Amendment does not merely protect sport shooting and hunting, though it clearly does that.

Nor does the Second Amendment exist to protect the Government's right to bear arms.

The framers of our Constitution wrote the Second Amendment with a greater purpose.

They made the Second Amendment the law of the land because it has something very particular to say about the rights of every man and every woman, and about the relationship of every man and every woman to his or her Government.

That is, the first right of every human is the right of self-defense.

Let me repeat that.

The first right of every human being is the right of self-defense. Without that right, all other rights are meaningless. The right of self-defense is not something the Government bestows upon its citizens. It is an inalienable right, older than the Constitution itself. It existed prior to the social contract of our Constitution. It is a right that Government did not create and therefore it is a right the government simply cannot take away. The framers of our Constitution understood this clearly. Therefore, they did not merely acknowledge that the right exists. They denied Congress the power to infringe upon that right.

Under the social contract that is the Constitution of the United States, the American people have told Congress explicitly that we do not have the authority to abolish the American people's rights to defend themselves. Further, the framers said [that] not only does the Congress not have the power to abolish that right, but Congress may not even infringe upon that right.

That is what the Second Amendment clearly lays out. Our Founding Fathers wrote the Second Amendment to tell us that a free state cannot exist if the people are denied the right or the means to defend themselves.

This is the meaning of the Second Amendment. Over the years, a lot of our citizens and many politicians have tried to nudge that definition around. But contrary to what the media and the President say, the right to keep and bear arms is as important today as it was 200 years ago.

Every day in this country thousands of peaceful, law-abiding Americans use guns to defend themselves, their families, and their property. Oftentimes, complete strangers are protected by the citizen who steps up and stops the thief or the stalker or the rapist or the murderer.

According to the FBI, criminals used guns in 1998 380,000 times across America. Yet research indicates that peaceful, law-abiding Americans, using their constitutional right, used guns to prevent 2.5 million crimes in America in that year and nearly every year. In fact, I believe the benefits of protecting the people's right to keep and bear arms far outweighs the destruction wrought by criminals and firearms accidents.

The Center[s] for Disease Control report 32,000 Americans died from firearm injuries in 1997; under any estimate, that is a tragedy. Unfortunately, the Center[s] for Disease Control do not keep track of the number of lives that were saved when guns were used in a defensive manner.

Yet if we were to survey the public every year, we would find [that] 400,000 Americans report they used a gun in a way that almost certainly saved either their life or somebody else's life.

Is that estimate too high? Perhaps.

I hope it is, because every time a life is saved from violence, that means that someone was threatening a life with violence. But that number would have to be over thirteen times too high for our opponents to be correct when they say that guns are used to kill more than they are used to protect. What they have been saying here and across America simply isn't true and the facts bear that out.

We are not debating the tragedy. We are debating facts at this moment. They cannot come up with 2.5 million gun crimes. But clearly, through surveys, we can come up with 2.5 million crimes thwarted every year when someone used a gun in defense of themselves or their property. In many cases, armed citizens not only thwarted crime, but they held the suspect until the authorities arrived and placed that person in custody.

Stories of people defending themselves with guns do not make the nightly news. It just simply isn't news in America.

It isn't hot.

It isn't exciting.

It *is* American. Sometimes when people act in an American way, it simply isn't reportable in our country anymore. So the national news media don't follow it.

Yet two of the school shootings that have brought gun issues to the forefront in the last year, in Pearl, Mississippi, and Edinboro, Pennsylvania, were stopped by peaceful gun owners using their weapons to subdue the killer until the police arrived.

How did that get missed in the story?

It was mentioned once, in passing, and then ignored as people ran to the floor of the Senate to talk about the tragedy of the killings. Of course, the killings were a tragedy. But it was also heroic that someone used their Constitutional right to save lives in the process.

A third school shooting in Springfield, Oregon, was stopped because some parents took time to teach their child the wise use of guns. So when the young man heard a particular sound coming from the gun, he was able to rush the shooter because he knew the gun had run out of ammunition. He was used to guns. He was around them. He subdued the shooter and potentially saved many other lives. We have recognized him nationally for that heroic act, that young high school student in Springfield, Oregon.

For some reason, my colleagues on the other side of the aisle never want to tell these stories. They only want to say, after such a crisis, "Pass a new gun control law and call 911." Yet these stories are essential to our understanding of the rights of the people to keep and bear arms.

I will share a few of these stories right now. Shawnra Pence, a 29-year-old mother from Sequim, Washington, home alone with one of her children, heard an intruder break into her house. She took her 9mm (handgun) and her child into the bedroom. When the 18-year-old criminal broke into the bedroom, she said, "Get out of my house. I have a gun. Get out now!" He left and the police caught him. She saved her life and her child's life. It made one brief story in the *Peninsula Daily News* [of the Olympic Peninsula in] Washington.

We have to talk about these stories because it is time America heard the other side of this debate. There are 2.5 million Americans out there defending themselves and their property by the use of their Constitutional right.

In Cumberland, Tennessee, 28-year-old Jason McCulley broke into the home of Stanley Horn and his wife, tied up the couple at knifepoint, and demanded to know where the couple kept some cash. While Mrs. Horn was directing the robber, Mr. Horn wriggled free from his restraints, retrieved his handgun, and shot the intruder, then called the police. The intruder subsequently died.

If some Senators on the other side of the aisle had their way, perhaps the Horns would have been killed and Jason McCulley would have walked away.

Earlier today, we heard the Senator from Illinois and the Senator from California read the names of people killed by guns in America. Some day they may read the name Jason McCulley. I doubt they will tell you how he died, however, because it doesn't advance their goal of destroying the Second Amendment. But, as Paul Harvey would say: Now you know the rest of the story.

Every thirteen seconds this story is repeated across America. Every thirteen seconds someone uses a gun to stop a crime. Why do our opponents never tell these stories? Why do the enemies of the right to keep and bear arms ignore this reality? Why is it that all we hear from them is, "Pass a new gun control law, and, by the way, call 911"?

I encourage all [who are] listening today, if you have heard of someone using their Second Amendment rights to prevent a crime, to save a life, to protect another life, then send us your story. There are people here who desperately need to hear this in Washington, right here on Capitol Hill. This is a story that should be played out every day in the press but isn't.

So let's play it out, right here on the floor of the Senate. Send me those stories from your local newspapers about that law-abiding citizen who used his constitutional right of self-defense. Send that story to me, or send it to your own Senator. Let him or her know the rest of the story of America's constitutional rights.

Having said all of this, let there be no mistake. Guns are not for everyone. We restrict children's access to guns and we restrict criminals' access to guns. But we must not tolerate politicians who tell us that the Second Amendment only protects the right to hunt. We must not tolerate politicians who infringe upon our right to defend ourselves from thieves and stalkers and rapists and murderers. And we must not tolerate the politician who simply says, "Pass another gun control law and call 911."

Senator Larry D. Craig
520 Hart Senate Office Building
Washington, DC 20510
Telephone: 202-224-2752
Fax: 202-228-1067

Preface

Fate reversal.

It's what didn't happen that could have happened.

While researching this book, it struck me that armed citizens have altered history time and again. How many of us are walking around unharmed because someone with a firearm intervened to spare us the trauma of being robbed, assaulted, raped, or even murdered? In many cases, we aren't aware that we were saved.

On November 18, 1998, a serial rapist was shot dead by his intended victim near the campus of the University of North Carolina-Charlotte.

At 3:00 a.m., Adrian Rodricka Cathey jimmied a sliding glass door and entered the woman's apartment. Once in her bedroom, he used a knife to control his victim as he attempted to rape her. But during the assault, the unidentified co-ed reached into a nightstand beside her bed, found her pistol, and blasted four holes into Cathey's chest.

He stumbled from the house and collapsed in the parking lot.

His death solved a mystery.

For nearly a year, a serial rapist had terrorized students of the University of North Carolina-Charlotte. After his death, DNA results linked the assailant to four other rapes in the area.

Cathey was among the most dangerous of sexual predators, what criminologists call a "sadistic rapist," one who obtains gratification through the suffering of his victims. Although Adrian Rodricka Cathey was never considered a suspect in the rapes until after his death, he had a history of violence against women. In October 1995, he'd been arrested on three counts of attempted murder and rape, but the charges were later dropped. In 1996, he was arrested for assault, but again, the charges were dismissed.

A week after Cathey died, Jack Clairbourne, the UNCC Associate Vice Chancellor for University Relations, issued a statement. "The university community," he said, "is glad that menace is relieved."

Research has shown that serial rapists average committing at least twenty sexual assaults before being captured. In this case, the co-ed who killed Cathey may have saved more than a dozen women from being raped or murdered.

Undoubtedly, many women still residing in Charlotte are unaware that they might have become victims of a violent assault had not an unsung heroine stopped Adrian Rodricka Cathey.

Many of these women may favor severe restrictions on gun ownership, never realizing that they are unknowing recipients of the collateral benefits of firearms.

On the night of March 21, 1995, a Little Rock, Arkansas, woman shook her husband awake.

"Someone's trying to break into our house," Jacqueline Wilburd whispered.

Mark Wilburd reached under the bed and grabbed his .38-caliber revolver. Then he rushed to the doorway of his bedroom.

"I heard a big crash," he later told jurors. Three intruders had kicked in his front door. Seconds later, a masked man charged down the hall toward him.

The man brandished a handgun and screamed, "LITTLE ROCK POLICE DEPARTMENT! HIT THE FLOOR!"

As his wife frantically tried to dial 911, Mark Wilburd faced a critical decision. Should he shoot an intruder who had identified himself as a police officer?

Fortunately, the choice was made for him.

"I saw fire coming from his gun," Wilburd said. A bullet blazed by his ear. Another thumped into the door jamb beside him.

Wilburd returned fire, then watched with relief as the gunman staggered, turned, and limped back down the hall.

Less than an hour later, two accomplices dropped Thomas Lamont Everett off at Southwest Hospital with a gunshot wound to the abdomen. Although he spent several days in critical condition, Everett survived. His partners were identified, and the three were convicted of attempted capital murder and armed robbery. They were subsequently sentenced to long prison sentences.

How many innocent victims were saved by the actions of the Arkansas homeowner?

The *Little Rock Democrat-Gazette* reported that the attempted robbery of Mark and Jacqueline Wilburd was the twenty-seventh home invasion in Little Rock in the previous six months. The attacks were becoming progressively more violent.

After Wilburd shot Everett, home invasions in Little Rock ended for more than a year. Police spokesman Terry Hastings said, "Since the March shooting, the robberies have virtually stopped."

Little Rock police believe that the co-defendants were responsible for the majority of the home invasions. Other local criminals, apparently seeing the danger of such methods of robbery, also stopped committing them.

This was another example of crimes that will never be committed because a citizen fought back with a gun.

In many cases, the armed citizen thwarts a crime just by the fact that the criminal sees or suspects he is armed. The intended victim may not even know that he has saved his own life.

On Wednesday evening, October 15, 1998, 78-year-old Gerald Leary and his wife Carol were watching *Wheel of Fortune* in their upscale Pinellas County, Florida, home. When they heard a knock on the door, Gerald got up to open it.

Two men forced their way inside.

The intruders held the couple at gunpoint, bound them, and ransacked the home. After stealing money and jewelry, they forced the couple into the garage and placed them in the trunk of their own car.

The assailants, trailed by two female companions in a second car, drove eighty miles north. When they saw a state trooper sitting in his cruiser alongside the road, they panicked and abandoned the Leary car in a heavily wooded area near Belleview, Florida.

According to the *St. Petersburg Times*, "The Learys waited [for] hours in the trunk, terrified that they would not be found. They drank drops of condensation from inside the trunk to quench their thirst."

Finally, a homeowner spotted the abandoned car and called police. When a deputy arrived, he heard Gerald Leary tapping on the inside of the trunk with a golf ball. The deputy then rescued the dehydrated couple from their terrifying ordeal.

But the Learys weren't Marty Lee Lunsford and Gregory Royster's first choice of victims.

A few minutes before these career burglars invaded the Leary home, they knocked on the door of another nearby dwelling. The homeowner became suspicious of the scruffy-looking pair and lifted his shirt to show them a handgun. They quickly left.

Because he merely displayed a handgun, the first intended victim undoubtedly saved himself and his wife, who was also home at the time. Had the home invasion and kidnapping of the Learys never occurred, the armed homeowner would have been unaware that he saved himself and his wife from a horrifying ordeal.

His act of self-defense would never have been known.

The above are three of thousands of cases I found in which armed citizens successfully defended themselves and others.

For this book, I interviewed more than two dozen victims who fought back against brutal criminal assaults. By their actions, they not only saved their own lives and property, but unknowingly saved the lives and property of many others.

Recent studies have confirmed that more than 75 percent of violent crimes are committed by criminals with a history of arrests and incarceration. When an armed citizen stops a violent attack — either by killing the assailant, incapacitating him, or causing the felon to be arrested — the citizen may well have saved scores of potential victims from violent assault, robbery, or even murder. If, as Professor Gary Kleck of Florida State University believes, hundreds of thousands of assaults, robberies, burglaries, rapes, and murders are stopped each year by armed citizens, many of those acts of self-defense also save others from being attacked. In at least 98 percent of these cases, a shot is never fired. Once an assailant sees that his victim is armed, the inclination is to flee. Because of the fear many law-abiding citizens have of becoming enmeshed in a litigious and punitive criminal justice system, many cases of armed self-defense are never reported.

Kleck is one of the leading researchers on guns and violence in America. In his 1997 book *Targeting Guns: Firearms and Their Control (Social Institutions and Social Change)*, he argues that most gun control laws accomplish little. The use of firearms by law-abiding citizens, however, may prevent more than two million crimes each year.

Professor John Lott, of the University of Chicago, is even more explicit in his 1998 book, *More Guns, Less Crime: Understanding Crime and Gun Control Laws (Studies in Law and Economics)*. Lott's research has conclusively documented the fact that counties in the U.S. which have enacted "shall issue" concealed-carry permit laws have experienced a dramatic reduction in crime, whereas most counties which do not allow citizens to carry concealed weapons have seen an increase in crime. ("Shall issue" laws give law enforcement officials no choice — any citizen who qualifies for a license cannot be denied.) His conclusion is that if all states and counties had concealed-carry laws, more than 1,000 murders and 4,000 rapes would be prevented each year.

Because of its local nature, instances of self-defense rarely make national headlines. Like automobile accidents, which take a multi-car disaster to become national news, only the most shocking self-defense shootings (such as when Bernard Goetz shot four thugs who tried to rob him) ever receive national coverage. This makes such cases among the most under-reported stories in America.

In my previous book, *The Best Defense: True Stories of Intended Victims Who Defended Themselves With a Firearm*, I described a classic case of fate reversal.

For fifteen years, Doug and Judy Stanton had been stalked by a man obsessed with Judy. As Jerry Hessler's life deteriorated, he snapped. On the evening of November 19, 1995, he went on a rampage, intending to murder everyone whom he perceived had done him wrong.

He drove to the house of two former co-workers and shot them along with their 5-month-old child. As they lay dying, Hessler continued his spree, murdering the father of a female acquaintance who had spurned him. He also shot and wounded two more former co-workers.

Later that night, he arrived at the Stantons' Ashland, Ohio, home armed with a 9mm semiautomatic pistol.

As Hessler kicked in the door, Doug Stanton instructed his wife and four children to lie face-down on the floor. In the shootout that followed, Stanton wounded Hessler, ending his killing spree. The gunman was arrested while attempting to flee the scene. He was later convicted of four murders. Hessler currently sits on Ohio's death row.

In addition to the six members of the Stanton family who would have died that night had Doug Stanton not been armed, Hessler carried a list of eight additional former co-workers and acquaintances he intended to kill.

After the shootout, Doug Stanton said, "People are quick to espouse the virtues of gun restrictions. [They say] 'If it saves one life, it will be worth it.' Because the Stanton family had a gun, six lives were saved. Had there been restrictions on gun ownership, the Stantons would be dead. That is a fact, not a hypothetical situation!"

Stanton was being modest. In addition to saving his own family, he likely saved the lives of at least eight other innocent people that night.

This book was written for those who refused to become victims. Through their efforts to save themselves, they prevented suffering for countless others.

All the accounts described are documented through newspaper articles, police reports, court documents, and interviews with many of the intended victims. I have also spoken with law enforcement officials concerning many of these cases.

My own research has confirmed that there are thousands of cases of armed self-defense in this country each year. My ever-growing database currently consists of more than six thousand documented cases.

In addition to saving their own lives, how many additional thousands of innocent victims were saved by those six thousand armed citizens?

How many of those criminals never assaulted or raped or robbed or murdered you or me, or someone we know?

How many dark destinies were reversed because a would-be victim had access to a firearm?

Chapter One
Point Blank

"Why'd you shoot me, bitch?" Last words of home invader Shaarod Profitt, September 18, 1998.

It was a cool fall evening in Little Rock, Arkansas, when Don Mosely heard the storm door rattling. Thinking his brother was outside, the sixty-year-old, disabled homeowner walked to the door and opened it.

A masked man stood on the porch. He wore dark clothes and a black stocking mask knotted at the top. Holes had been cut out for his eyes and mouth. "Just like you see on television," Mosely later recalled.

He had little time to react.

The man pointed a gun at Mosely and demanded, "Gimme your car keys!"

When Mosely didn't respond, the assailant raised the barrel of the gun and stuck it in the homeowner's face.

"Gimme your keys!" he ordered again.

In a recent interview, Mosely recalled, "He had a .22-caliber Marlin semiautomatic rifle. He'd cut the stock off and made a pistol grip. I grabbed the barrel of the gun and his first shot hit the door facing. We wrestled around and I almost got it away from him. But he ended up shooting me."

Doctors later determined that the bullet, which had been fired point blank into his stomach, had careened down into. Mosely's right thigh. Although he felt little pain, his leg went numb, and he fell to the floor.

The suddenness of the attack stunned Mosely. He decided to play dead, hoping the intruder wouldn't shoot him again.

Lying still, he thought of the gun he'd hidden beside his chair. If he could get to it, he might be able to stop the assailant.

Just moments before the stranger had appeared at their door, Mosely and his wife, Jane, had returned home after dining at a local restaurant with Don's brother. While Don settled down in his rocker, Jane grabbed a bowl of cereal from the kitchen and walked back into the bedroom.

When he heard the door rattling, Don assumed it was his brother coming back to the house to pick up something he'd left.

Don and Jane Mosely had lived in the comfortable home on Richland Drive for thirty-nine years. The couple had raised their children there, but their memories belied today's reality. In the last few years, they'd watched helplessly as the neighborhood changed. Now gang members lurked on street corners selling drugs and looking for trouble. Neighbors who used to wave or stop to chat now quickly disappeared into their own residences.

Even though times had changed, Jane, who was known by the children in the community as "Mom," still provided candy and cakes as treats to the neighborhood children. She always had a ready smile for those trapped in the bleak surroundings.

Now the thug stood over Don Mosely, as if deciding whether to shoot again.

At that moment, Mosely heard a thud in the bedroom.

The intruder also heard it and suddenly sprinted away. Don raised his head and saw the man disappear down the hall.

He was headed straight toward the bedroom!

Oh my God, he thought. This guy's gonna kill my wife.

Mosely pulled himself to his feet. But he fell when he tried to walk. He stood again. After a few minutes, he found that if he dragged his leg behind him, he could maneuver enough to get around.

He was surprised he wasn't bleeding more. A smear of blood about the size of a silver dollar spotted the floor where he'd lain.

"I had a little American Arms .22-caliber Magnum revolver," he said. "It was sitting beside my chair. I picked it up, but my leg wouldn't work very well. Before I could get all the way back there, I could already hear them shooting."

Jane Mosely had been sitting on the edge of the bed eating her cereal. She'd turned on the television and placed the telephone beside her. When she heard Don get up and go to the door, she also thought that her husband's brother had returned.

"But when I heard a stranger's voice at the door, I knew something was wrong," Jane recalled in a recent interview. "So I picked up the phone and dialed 911. Then I heard the shots and heard my husband moan. I thought he was dead. That's when I crossed the room to get my gun out of the closet."

The couple usually kept their .32-caliber Smith & Wesson snub-nosed revolver beside the bed. But because their grandchildren had been visiting recently, Jane had placed it on a shelf in the closet.

She figured it would only be a matter of time before the intruder headed for the bedroom.

After retrieving the gun, Jane sought refuge behind a chest of drawers in the back corner of the room. It seemed to offer at least some protection.

Jane muttered a quick prayer and waited for the gunman to appear. Crouched behind the chest of drawers, she followed his shadow as it moved across the doorway.

His appearance startled her. With his black mask, his dark clothes, and lithe figure, he reminded her of a ninja warrior.

Then she saw the gun.

She was still talking to the dispatcher when he entered the room. But as soon as she saw him, Jane threw the phone on the floor. She later learned that the entire gunfight had been recorded on the 911 tape.

The masked intruder edged cautiously into the room.

As soon as he saw Jane, he fired.

The shot slammed into the chest of drawers, causing the housewife to flinch.

Jane recalled, "He had to come pretty far into the room to be able to shoot me because I was backed up in the corner and had some protection from the chest of drawers. When he saw me, he spun around and aimed his gun at me. Then we both started shooting at each other. Police later said he fired eleven shots. I don't have any recollection of how many shots I fired. I don't remember when I was hit in the arm, but I did feel the bullet that hit me in the groin."

She aimed at his head and pressed the trigger. The blast deafened her.

The small bedroom had become a war zone. The gunman's volleys thudded into the wall behind her. A television that sat on the chest of drawers took a direct hit — the glass shattered, stinging her face. The intruder continued to move toward Jane, still shooting.

The first time she was hit, Jane felt panic surge up inside her. But she knew she had to remain calm. She fired again, and continued to pull the trigger until the gun no longer fired.

Chapter One
Point Blank

Jane remembered, "He kept coming closer and closer, firing all the time. There was a little stool in front of the dresser, and he crouched behind that stool. He was constantly raising up and shooting at me."

By now, Jane's revolver was empty. She continued squeezing the trigger, only to hear it clicking into an empty chamber.

She was bleeding, and the pain in her abdomen was excruciating.

Now her assailant was just a few feet away. She could see that she had hit him at least twice — blood pumped from an open wound to his throat, and his mask had turned crimson.

He held the rifle as if it were a pistol. It was then that, like her husband, she noticed the stock had been cut off and carved like a pistol grip.

The man seemed determined to kill her, like some madman in a cheap stalker movie. She was bleeding heavily. If I get shot again, Jane thought, I'm dead.

By now, the gunman had closed the distance to less than a foot. In desperation, Jane flung her empty gun to the floor, and grabbed the barrel of his rifle.

The gunman tried to wrench it away, and the two combatants fell to the floor. He landed on top of her and somehow squeezed off another round. The bullet missed Jane and plowed into the floor. The assailant attempted to twist the barrel into her torso so that he could shoot her again, but the fear of dying drove her to push it away.

The struggle lasted for about two minutes. But it seemed like forever to Jane Mosely.

She thought of her children.

I will *not* die, she thought. I *will* survive.

Don Mosely later recalled the horrific scene he saw when he entered the bedroom.

"When I got back there," he said, "[the gunman] and my wife were on the floor in the damnedest puddle of blood you've ever seen. They were struggling for the gun — he kept trying to point the barrel towards my wife, and she kept pushing it back."

The stool had been knocked to the floor, and a lamp had shattered. Bullet holes dotted the walls, and splinters of wood from the chest of drawers lay on the floor.

But what struck Mosely was the complete silence as the two fought desperately for the gun.

He dragged his lame leg toward them, using the bedpost to help steady himself.

By now the gunman was straddling Jane. She lay on her back, still holding onto the sawed-off rifle.

When Don Mosely was less than a foot from the assailant, he placed the pistol against the man's head.

At point-blank range, the homeowner pulled the trigger. At the crack of the gunshot, the invader dropped to his knees. He loosened his grip on the rifle, allowing Jane to wrench it from him.

Don cocked the gun and fired again. The man's body went limp, and he collapsed to the floor.

Jane Mosely lay in the corner of the room where she'd made her stand. Her dress was stained crimson, and now her body ached all over. But she was jubilant to see that her husband had survived.

The gunman lay beside her, gasping, blood still pumping out of the wound in his neck.

Don Mosely recalled, "I grabbed his gun and threw it up on the bed. Then I picked up the phone, and told the dispatcher we'd both been shot."

Blood from Jane and the intruder flowed to form a pool on the floor.

She thought the masked man was dead. But he slowly raised his head. Twisting toward Jane, he asked, "Why'd you shoot me, bitch?" They were the last words Shaarod Profitt ever said.

` Jane later recalled that she was incredulous that he would ask such a question. Although she didn't respond, she thought, why do you think I shot you?

Police had been instructed by dispatchers to treat the call as a domestic disturbance. Don Mosely, standing in the hall, still held his gun when the first officers arrived. He was ordered to put his weapon down, then he was forced to the floor and handcuffed.

Investigators at the scene quickly determined what had happened. The handcuffs were removed, and Don Mosely was examined by paramedics. Unlike the gunman and his wife, he'd bled very little.

The wounded homeowners were placed on stretchers and rushed to local hospitals. Both Jane Mosely and the intruder, identified as teenager Shaarod Profitt, were transported to Baptist Hospital, while Don was sent to University Hospital.

During exploratory surgery, Don developed a staph infection and had to be hospitalized several times before recuperating. Jane Mosely spent five days in the hospital, but eventually recovered completely.

Shaarod Profitt died the following day.

After a lengthy investigation, police arrested a second suspect, Tyrone Cooper, and charged him with being an accomplice. Through interviews with Cooper and other witnesses, investigators put together the following sequence of events that led to the foiled home invasion.

Profitt, Cooper, and an unidentified gang member had seen Don Mosely driving a new Chrysler LHS and decided to steal it.

Dressed in dark clothing and masks, they walked up to the porch. Just as they were about to kick in the door, Don Mosely opened it. Almost immediately, he began to fight for his life with the gunman. Profitt's accomplices fled as soon as the first shot was fired.

A neighbor had seen the strange trio walk up onto the steps to the Mosely home and called police. The witness recognized Profitt and Cooper but not the third robber.

Witnesses pointed out a house that Cooper had entered and he was quickly arrested. A mask, duct tape, and a knife were found in a yard nearby.

He later plea-bargained a sentence of twenty-five years in prison. By law, Cooper must serve all of his sentence without the possibility of parole.

Not surprisingly, Don and Jane Mosely take gun ownership seriously. In a recent interview, Jane said, "I think everybody ought to be able to own guns and I don't think people should be forced to put trigger locks on them. I know if there had been one on the gun I used, I wouldn't be here. I'm also against having to register your guns. I just think they're taking too much of our freedom away. [Our family has] always had guns, and we taught our children how to use guns safely."

She paused, and said, "Thank God we knew how to protect ourselves."

Chapter One
Point Blank

9

Don concurred. "My wife and I used to go out every weekend and target practice with handguns," he said. He states that he believes the Federal and state governments do not have the right to pass gun control legislation.

Don also has his own theory about why he and Jane were shot.

"If [Profitt] didn't intend to kill us," he said, "why didn't he leave after shooting me instead of going back to the bedroom after my wife? They planned to kill both of us to get the car. It might have even been a gang initiation. But I know he came in here with murder on his mind."

Both Don and Jane Mosely agree that had they not owned firearms they would both be dead. And they wonder how many other victims would have died at the hands of Profitt and Cooper had they been allowed to continue their lives of crime.

Don and Jane Mosely recently moved to a new neighborhood to be closer to their children and grandchildren. They feel safe there. But they still keep their guns ready. Just in case.

Chapter Two
School Shooting

"Why? Why? Why are you killing my kids?" Joel Myrick, Assistant Principal of Pearl, Mississippi, High School. October 1, 1997.

Luke Woodham swung the aluminum baseball bat with all the strength he could muster. He was no athlete, too chubby and uncoordinated, but he put all his power into this swing. His mother, Mary, never saw it coming. The bat cracked squarely against her jaw.

Woodham thought she would fall, but instead, she staggered back against the kitchen sink. He glared at the woman he hated. Blood pumped in angry spurts from her mouth. Shattered bone and teeth dotted the floor beneath her. She tried to speak, but only managed to gurgle something unintelligible.

The one-story, ranch-style house seemed like a prison to the sixteen-year-old. He attended Pearl High School, and held a part-time job at a local Domino's Pizza. But unless he was working or at school, he rarely left the house. This morning, however, Woodham planned to make history. He would forever commit his soul to the dark side.

His mother stood in shocked silence, swaying against the sink. Woodham yanked a butcher knife from a kitchen drawer. It had a twelve-inch, serrated blade.

Suddenly, his mother darted away. Woodham followed, watching as she stumbled down the hall and into her bedroom.

The door slammed in his face, but one swing of the bat knocked it off its hinges. The enraged teenager kicked it the rest of the way open and entered.

His mother cowered at the foot of her bed. He slashed at her, but she stood and threw up her hands to protect herself. The blade gouged deep gashes in her forearms, drawing more blood. Again and again, the crazed teenager lashed out at his mother.

Finally, she crumpled onto the bed. Woodham straddled her, placed a pillow over her head, and continued plunging the knife deep into his mother's body. How could this bitch have controlled him for so long?

After several minutes, Woodham was exhausted.

Breathing heavily, he stood up. He walked to the kitchen sink and washed his hands. When he finished, the teen saw that his palms were bleeding. He figured his hands must have slipped down onto the blade as he stabbed his mother. In his angry attack, he hadn't even noticed. Woodham reached beneath the counter, found a roll of black duct tape, and wrapped his wounds.

The kitchen floor, the sink, and the counters were smeared with blood. Crimson streaks painted the walls and ceiling.

Woodham pulled a dishtowel from a drawer and began to wipe down the walls. But after a few minutes he decided it was futile.

Pearl High School would open in about two hours, at eight o'clock. Looking outside, Woodham saw the dawn breaking. The excitement of what he was about to do gripped him.

He thought about his dog, Sparkle. Two days earlier, he'd killed it. Woodham and other members of The Kroth had stuck knives into its hide to torture it. They'd laughed as the little dog shrieked. Finally, they poured gasoline down the throat of the dog and lit it. The writhing and desperate howls of the dog had set the stage for today. After killing the animal, Woodham knew he could kill his mother.

He walked into his bedroom and changed clothes. Then he sat at his desk, took out a pen and pad, and began to compose a final note.

"I am not insane," he wrote. "I am angry... I am not spoiled or lazy for murder is not [for the] weak and slow-witted. Murder is gutsy and daring. I killed because people like me are mistreated everyday. I do this to show society 'push us and we will push back!' I suffered all my life. No one ever truly loved me. No one ever truly cared for me. I only loved one thing in my whole life and that was Christina Menefee. But she was torn away from me. I tried to save myself with Melissa Williams, but she never cared for me. As it turns out, she made fun of me behind my back while we were together. And all throughout my life I was ridiculed. Always beaten, always hated. Can you, society, truly blame me for what I do? Yes, you will, the ratings wouldn't go high enough if you didn't and it wouldn't make good gossip for all the old ladies. But I shall tell you one thing. I am malicious because I am miserable. The world has beat on me. Wednesday, October 1, 1997, shall go down in history as the day I fought back..."

When he finished with the note, Woodham stuffed it into his pocket.

He pulled a blue trench coat over his clothes and took a .30-30 Marlin lever-action deer rifle from his brother's closet. Checking to make sure it was loaded, the teenager dumped two boxes of ammunition into his pocket. Then he walked out to his mother's car.

Woodham didn't have a driver's license, so when she was alive, his mother wouldn't let him drive. Another way, he thought, that the bitch controlled his every move. He threw the rifle onto the seat, cranked up the engine, and drove away.

It was exactly 8:06 a.m.

Joel Myrick, assistant principal of Pearl High School, watched students filing into the school.

Joel Myrick

"There's a large area where the kids gather before school," Myrick stated in a recent interview. "It's called the 'commons.' At lunchtime, we roll tables out for the kids to eat on, but in the mornings it's a large, open area with a forty-foot-high ceiling and is about seventy feet wide. Probably five or six hundred kids were already there, just milling around, talking."

Holding a cup of coffee, Myrick walked toward his office. As he opened the door, he heard an explosion.

"It sounded like a cannon," he said.

Myrick was confused. He wondered if the roof was caving in.

There was a second explosion, followed by screams.

Suddenly, a panicked stream of teenagers was running toward his office. Still not sure of what was happening, Myrick shuttled them through the door. As he did so, he noticed a mass of students scrambling toward the exits. His office quickly filled up with sobbing, shaking teenagers.

By that time, the unthinkable was beginning to seep into his consciousness.

A veteran hunter, Myrick owned several guns, including high-powered rifles. He knew the damage they could do. He began to realize that someone might be hunting his kids.

"It all happened in a matter of just a few seconds," Myrick remembered. "I turned and started walking toward the commons, crouching and looking to see what was going on. About that time I heard another shot, and concrete splattered off the column in the center of the commons. Then I saw a girl go down."

Myrick concluded that someone definitely was shooting students, but a stairwell blocked his view of much of the commons so he still hadn't seen the shooter.

Myrick recalled, "I made my way out into the commons trying to get a good view. At that point I saw the muzzle of a rifle. Then I saw the boy, a large kid with a long coat on. I could tell that the gun he had was a .30-30 lever-action rifle. He was walking out into the commons and shot a girl who was standing next to the center column. She went down and I thought, my God, he's killing kids in the school. It was such a foreign concept that I was filled with disbelief for a moment. My next thought was, what can I do?"

Myrick watched the teenager stroll toward another column. Three students were hiding behind it. As the shooter walked around the edge, one of the students placed his backpack in front of his chest and yelled, "No, man, no!"

The shooter, Luke Woodham (Myrick had seen him around the campus but didn't remember his name), lowered the rifle and shot the student through the pelvis.

When the other two students ran, Woodham wheeled about, turned in their direction, and snapped off two quick shots. The bullets ricocheted off the floor and bounced like shrapnel, slicing into the students' legs. Both fell, and lay writhing on the floor.

Most of the teenagers had fled down the hall and out of the building, but some were frozen in place. These were the students the shooter was targeting.

Myrick's first thought was to charge the gunman and attempt to subdue him. But there was a space of about sixty feet between them. The assistant principal knew he would be killed before he could even get close.

Myrick recalled, "When he finished shooting, he reached into his pocket and started thumbing .30-30 rounds into the magazine. Then he turned and started walking toward the hallway entrance. I knew my gun was in my truck, so I started to what I call 'lightfooting' it out into the commons. I had to get out to my truck. I tried to remain as quiet as possible. He kept his back turned to me. When he [opened the door] and entered the hallway, I saw bodies laying around everywhere, and I heard moaning and screaming. He walked away with the rifle at port-arms across his chest. The image froze in my mind."

Then Woodham turned and saw Myrick looking at him.

The assistant principle gave up any pretense at stealth and sprinted across the commons, away from the crazed youth. He was surprised when he made it to the parking area without being shot. Myrick raced to his truck, keys already in hand. He unlocked the door and tore it open. The assistant principal reached into the map pocket and grabbed his pistol, a Colt 1991 A1 Compact Model .45 semiautomatic.

Myrick kept six rounds in the magazine, but none in the chamber. He racked the slide and watched as the top bullet was mechanically stripped from the magazine and fed into the chamber.

The gravity of what he was doing devastated Myrick.

He recalled, "For just a split second after it registered, I got a sinking feeling. I thought, 'Oh my God, I've just chambered a live round on school property.'"

Myrick started running toward the door where he thought the gunman might exit. "I was headed toward the door," he remembered, "and was thinking, 'I'm going to go through the door ready to shoot. I'm going to hear the gunshots and the screams, and I'm going to go down the hall to where the shooter is, and I'm going to do my best to stop it.'"

But when Myrick got about thirty yards from the door, Woodham walked out. "His rifle was half-up in the ready position," Myrick remembered.

Myrick, running now as fast as he could, slid to a stop.

The two looked at each other for a moment, then the assistant principal assumed a shooter's stance, aimed his gun at Woodham, clicked off the safety, and yelled, "Stop!"

The killer continued walking, at an angle to Myrick, toward the student parking lot. He acted as if he hadn't heard the warning.

Now Myrick was stymied.

He remembered, "Ever since I was a little boy, the backdrop behind my intended target had been drilled into my mind. [But here there] was no backdrop. There was a road, which he would later try to leave on, and there were kids — some students were coming to school and were unaware that anything had happened. Some kids were leaving and trying to run out, others were just standing around. So I didn't even try to shoot."

Myrick engaged the gun's manual safety and watched as Woodham walked deliberately to his car. It was a white mid-sized Chevrolet sedan.

"When I saw him open the door," Myrick recalled, "I took off and started running toward the one entrance to the school. I knew he was going to have to go down the circular drive to the stop sign and take a right. He boiled his tires as he took off, and I remember seeing white smoke. Then he headed straight for the stop sign."

Finally, Myrick's luck changed.

A car was parked at the stop sign, blocking Woodham's exit. This gave the assistant principal time to reach the gunman. Woodham began honking his horn at the car in front of him, but the driver never moved. Finally, the inexperienced driver backed up and screeched around the car.

Myrick said, "When he came around the car, I clicked my safety off and pointed my gun at him. My plan was that when he drove by, there would be a good backdrop, and I was going to try to shoot him."

When Woodham saw Myrick standing in the middle of the road with a gun trained on his car, he panicked. He swerved off the side of the road into a ditch. There was dew on the ground and when Woodham tried to come back up on the road, he lost control. His tires spun in the wet grass as he attempted to regain the road.

"He was ten feet across the road from me, looking straight at me," Myrick recalled. "When he stopped, I was looking right over the three dots of my pistol sights at him. I saw his glasses were askew, and his knuckles were just gleaming white. Both hands were on top of the steering wheel."

"FREEZE, OR I'LL BLOW YOUR HEAD OFF!"

Myrick sprinted to the side of the car. Looking inside, he saw the rifle on the seat beside Woodham. "First thing I noticed was that his hands were taped," Myrick recalled. It was one of the things that stuck in his mind long after the incident. The assistant principle wondered if the black tape was a gang sign, or a death symbol.

"Don't move!" Myrick shouted.

Woodham sat there, his eyes glazed over.

Using his left hand, Myrick opened the door and ordered the killer to get out. Woodham emerged from the car with his hands in the air.

Myrick commanded him to lie face down on the ground. The assistant principal remembered, "I straddled him and yanked his coat up, covering his head. I checked him for another gun or a knife, then eased the jacket back to where his head was exposed. Then I put my foot on the back of his neck. I stuck the barrel of the gun against the back of his head."

"Why?" Myrick asked. "Why? Why are you killing my kids?"

Woodham calmly replied, "Mr. Myrick, the world has wronged me. I just couldn't take it anymore."

The response enraged Myrick. "Yeah, just wait until you get to Parchman!" Myrick snapped, referring to Mississippi's infamous state penitentiary.

Myrick later recalled, "I just looked up at the sky and screamed in rage. It was crazy. I was standing there on the side of the road with some kid who'd just shot up the school. None of it made any sense."

Minutes later, a police cruiser pulled up. Pearl Police Department Officer Roy Dampier got out and drew his weapon.

"Is this the shooter?" he asked.

Myrick nodded.

"Who is it?" Dampier asked.

Myrick answered, "I don't know."

"Oh, you know me, Mr. Myrick," Woodham said. "I'm the guy that gave you the discount on the pizza the other night."

Myrick was amazed. While he vaguely recalled the incident, it had stuck in Woodham's mind.

Myrick stepped back and let Dampier take custody of Woodham.

"You got him?" the assistant principal asked.

"Yes, I've got him."

Myrick couldn't believe what had just happened. He'd seen students gunned down in the school. He'd seen the carnage, the panic, had felt the adrenalin of fear slam into him like a fist to the belly. Then, on school property, he'd pulled a gun on a student.

Deep down, he knew that something in America had changed. No one had ever shot up a school before. It made Myrick want to cry.

Now, still standing on the road, the assistant principal took the magazine out of his gun, then pocketed both.

Dreading what he was about to see, he sprinted back toward the school. Entering, he found the commons dark and deathly quiet. A dozen students lay scattered across the floor.

"I went up to the first student, and I saw a hole just below her Adam's apple. I reached down and touched her. She was dead. I said, 'God bless this child, God bless this child, God bless this child.' I said it three times. Then I turned and took about four steps over to the next student, whose eyes were fluttering. She'd been shot through the arm. The bullet went into her side and through the lungs. I straddled the girl and then her eyes stopped fluttering."

Myrick said another prayer, then looked around. His mind took in the blood-soaked floor and the students lying like wounded soldiers on a battlefield. He moved to another student lying a few feet away. She was conscious, but in shock. A fourth girl sat against the center column — a bullet had grazed her shoulder, and, though she was bleeding, her wound didn't seem to be life threatening.

Myrick then walked toward three more students. While he was checking them, someone said, "There's more in the band hall."

The assistant principal recalled, "I said, 'My God!' and took off running down to the band hall. There was a blood trail to follow there. I opened the door and saw that one boy had a pass-through wound in his calf, and a second student had a belly wound. They were being taken care of [by other teachers] at that point."

In total disbelief, Myrick walked out of the band hall and back outside. He stopped long enough to use his shoe to try to rub the blood puddles off the sidewalk. "It was a principal thing," he said. "Trying to keep the school clean."

He went back to his office, put his gun in his desk, and locked the door. By now he was in a daze. It seemed that something sacred had been broken, and he was grasping to try to understand.

He recalled, "I walked back outside. By now ambulances were everywhere. The police were coming in, and it was pandemonium. I looked up and saw a highway patrol officer crouched with an M-16. That's when I realized there could have been more than one shooter. There were twenty or thirty police cars, and the police had formed a kind of picket line keeping parents back. They were having a hard time keeping people out, which is understandable."

By now, all the students were gone. Authorities quickly loaded the teachers on a bus and took them to the police department for statements.

Myrick was concerned that he would be charged with carrying a weapon on school property. However, both the school superintendent and the police chief told him not to worry.

When interviewed by detectives, Woodham admitted to authorities that, when he ran out of victims at the high school, he planned to drive to the middle school, which was located less than a mile away, and shoot as many students and teachers as possible. Then he planned to kill himself. The more trophies he collected, the higher his standing in Hades, the afterlife.

During the subsequent investigation, police learned that several members of a satanic cult called "The Kroth" had planned the murders. Woodham, new to the cult, had been assigned to carry out the plan.

In addition to his mother, Woodham murdered Christina Menefee and Lydia Kaye Dew. He wounded seven other students.

Although the teenager hated his mother, family members and friends stated that she was a "typical mom." She wasn't a tyrant, didn't bring boyfriends home, and provided comfortably for her son.

In June 1998, Woodham was convicted of three counts of first-degree murder and seven counts of aggravated assault. He was given three life sentences, plus twenty years each for the aggravated assaults. (Authorities were unable to seek the death penalty because that sentence applies only to murders connected with another crime, such as robbery, burglary, or rape.)

Three other members of the Kroth were eventually convicted of various conspiracy charges.

Joel Myrick is now the principal of Corinth High School in Corinth, Mississippi. During a recent interview, he reflected on that day.

"It was a media circus," Myrick said. He appeared on several television shows, including CNN, NBC's *48 Hours*, and ABC's *20/20*. News media satellite trucks stayed in the small town for weeks, milking every drop of blood from the case.

"It's only been in the last few months that I've gotten on the side of the Second Amendment," Myrick said. "After every one of these school shootings, they try to pass more laws, and edge another six inches or so toward doing away with the Constitution."

Unlike many pro-gun advocates, Myrick feels that teachers should not be allowed to carry firearms on campus. "If the Constitution allows you to fly," he said, "you wouldn't fly unless you knew how. If the Constitution allows you the right to bear arms, there are different places where different levels of ability are necessary. The school is a fluid environment in which teachers are not there to be armed. It's not a good place for a teacher to carry a gun.

"However, I think there is no greater deterrent to these school shootings than for there to be a gun in the school. If we really value our kids' safety like we value our money in the banks, we would... hire someone in plain clothes with different types of weapons to be there on the school campus, like guards, or sentries. It should be somebody trained in the intricacies of schools that understand where the kids are, and help control access. But more importantly than anything [they would have to] be willing to give their own lives for the children."

Joel Myrick has received some criticism for taking a gun onto school property. But many students and parents are glad he did. They have no doubt that he saved dozens of lives by stopping Woodham.

Chapter Three
Occupational
Hazard

"It was a dreadful thing I had to do. Human life is precious to me. I hated to do it, but there was no other choice." Ann Barry, May 14, 1997.

The twenty-year-old Ford Granada was sagging. In addition to the woman at the wheel and two men crowded into the front seat, the rear was loaded with loot from earlier burglaries. VCRs. Bags filled with jewelry and guns and household items. Anything that could be easily sold for drugs.

It was Monday, May 12, 1997. This was to be just another heist for Tonya Marie Guntle, 26; James Shugart, 28; and Gordon W. Childress, 18.

They drove along Plum Springs Road, three miles north of Bowling Green, Kentucky. Bright-beam headlights guided the way. Guntle stayed well below the speed limit — she didn't need a state trooper pulling her over for some minor traffic violation.

"There it is," Childress said, pointing to a house in the distance. He'd scouted the area earlier. It was a ranch-style home with an enclosed garage. The house sat on a hill in the darkness, looking deserted.

A perfect target, Guntle thought. The only other house in sight had a "For Sale" sign out front and was obviously vacant. The mother of four had learned a lot since teaming up with Jimmy.

Guntle cut the lights, then glided into the driveway.

"Keep it running," Shugart ordered. "And keep your foot off the brake."

Her face reddened, and she was glad the men couldn't see. They'd almost been caught a few weeks earlier when Guntle had rested her foot on the brake during a burglary. Someone had seen the brake lights and called the cops. Fortunately, they were able to escape by using the back roads, but Shugart hadn't been happy.

He handed her a walkie-talkie. "Anybody comes down this road, let us know," he commanded.

Guntle nodded, then watched as the two men disappeared into the shadows.

Sweat beaded on her lips. They'd been knocking over houses for months now, and she kept thinking she'd get used to the knot in her gut. Jimmy had told her that nervous fear keeps you on your toes. Maybe, but she didn't like it.

Suddenly the walkie-talkie belched. Guntle jerked and her body became rigid. "We're in the garage," Jimmy said. "Now we gotta get in the house." He paused, then said, "They got it locked up tighter'n a drum!"

Then it was quiet again.

Guntle sat listening to the motor run. It had a loose rod, and the click-click-click was driving her insane.

The walkie-talkie sounded again. A series of heavy thuds almost knocked it out of her hand.

Jesus, she asked herself, what the hell are they doing?

After what seemed like an hour of hammering, Jimmy whispered into the radio. "We're in the house!" he breathed. "Had to ax down the door."

Guntle signed in relief. She glanced at her watch. It was exactly 11:00 p.m.

Chapter Three
Occupational Hazard

In a recent interview, Ann Barry, a professor at Western Kentucky University, recalled that evening.

Ann Barry

"I had just turned in my final grades," she remembered, "ending the spring semester, and felt as though I was suffering from battle fatigue. I went to bed at 9:30 and fell into a deep sleep."

Later, she heard a thump. Somewhere in her consciousness she thought she was having a nightmare. She turned over in her bed and drifted back to sleep.

A loud bang awakened her. She sat up in bed, her heart pounding. What's going on? she wondered.

The racket sounded like it came from outside, as if someone was chopping down a tree. Barry was wide awake now. She heard a splintering sound. It was then she realized that someone was battering down her door.

She later recalled, "You talk about a few minutes of sheer terror. My heart was frozen. I'm just grateful to God I could function."

Barry's first thought was to dial 911. But before she could grab her telephone she heard whispered voices inside her home.

Her heart pumped. Oh God, she thought, they're in the kitchen headed toward my bedroom.

Her grandfather had taught her to shoot a rifle when she was eight years old. She'd hunted with him when she was a child, but it was only recently she'd purchased a handgun.

In October 1996, the Kentucky Concealed Weapons Permit law went into effect. Although the law was opposed by such organizations as the Kentucky Association of Chiefs of Police, Barry had been active in lobbying her friends and associates to push for passage of the bill.

As a 60-year-old, single woman whose duties included teaching night courses, she felt the need for self-protection. Within weeks of the passage of the Concealed Permit law, Barry took the required course and received her license to carry a firearm.

"It's not something I did on a lark," she explained. "I take the responsibility very seriously."

Now Barry remembered the training she'd received. Remain calm, the instructors had drilled into her. Look for a way out. If there is one, run like hell to get away. Deadly force is to be used only as a last resort.

If there's no other way, don't panic.

But if you *must* shoot, shoot to kill.

"I thought, they're breaking down the door," Barry recalled. "They're coming to get me. I've only got a few seconds to think about what I'm going to have to do. I wanted to run, but there was no way out. I was trapped."

Chapter Three
Occupational Hazard

Barry kept a Ruger SP-101 .357 Magnum on her nightstand. The stainless-steel, 5-shot revolver was loaded with Hy-Shok cartridges, the same type used by many law enforcement officers in Bowling Green. These hollow-point bullets were designed to quickly stop a violent assailant.

She heard footsteps moving closer. Her heart was thumping so loudly that she thought the intruder could surely hear it.

Grabbing her gun, she cocked it and inched toward the hallway. Joe Brewer and Debbie Williams, her shooting instructors, had prepared Barry for just such a situation. Stay in the shadows, they had emphasized. Be silent, and let the invader come to you.

Now she saw the gunman. He held a pistol in his right hand. Was this the only intruder? she wondered.

"I had to seek a position to defend myself from whoever was coming toward my bedroom," Barry recalled. "Who? How many? My mind was frozen. I couldn't breathe. All I could do was take short, quick gasps... like a dog panting in the summer."

She watched the shadow move closer, then peer into the bedroom opposite hers.

The light snapped on, and she jumped.

Oh, God! Please help me, she prayed. The gunman was no more than three feet away. He glanced into the bedroom, then started to turn toward her.

It's now or never, Barry realized. If she didn't shoot now, the man would kill her. She stepped out of the doorway in order to position herself for the shot. Then she pointed the barrel toward his body and quickly pressed the trigger. The flash blinded her momentarily, and the percussion shook the little room. Suddenly, the hallway was filled with smoke.

The gunman shouted something unintelligible and reeled back against the opposite wall.

Barry jumped back into the darkness of her bedroom. It was just in the nick of time. "As soon as the bullet hit him," Barry said, "he swung around and started spraying bullets at me." Yellow flames rocketed from the barrel of his gun. Explosions deafened her. Bullets thudded into the walls within a few feet of her.

How could he miss? Barry wondered. He was less than five feet away.

She raised her gun to fire again, but the gunman abruptly turned and started back down the hall. Then he began to stagger, and she heard him crashing into furniture as he fled through the kitchen and back out into the garage.

She said, "I waited for what seemed like forever, until I felt sure that he was out of my house, and not lurking in the darkness waiting for me to emerge. Inching my way up the hall and finally peering from the kitchen door out through the garage windows, I could see lights on a vehicle where my driveway meets the road."

Barry picked up the telephone in the kitchen. Her hands were shaking so badly she could barely hold it. Her fingers punched at the numbers. After three tries, she finally managed to hit 911.

Outside, a scene was playing itself out that might have been comical in some other context.

Tonya Marie Guntle had heard several muffled pops inside the house, then watched Childress burst from the garage and sprint toward the car. He swung open the passenger door and dropped onto the seat.

"What the hell happened?" she asked.

Chapter Three
Occupational Hazard

Childress opened his mouth but no words came out.

"Where's Jimmy?"

As if in answer to her question, Shugart stumbled out of the garage. His legs wobbled, and he suddenly fell. Convulsing, as if he was having a seizure, he began to crawl toward the station wagon.

"Go help him!" Guntle ordered Childress.

Childress hesitated, then jumped out of the car and ran back across the lawn. He pulled the wounded man to his feet and dragged him to the car. After pushing Shugart into the back seat, Childress climbed in beside Guntle.

"Let's get outta here!" he screamed. His eyes were wide as he yelled, "Hit it!"

Guntle pulled the stick shift down, and the car suddenly rocketed backward.

"Take your foot off the gas!" Childress shouted. But it was too late. The car slammed to a stop in a ditch.

Shugart moaned. Guntle glanced into the back seat. She gagged when she saw a fist-sized hole in his side and blood pouring out of the wound onto the seat.

Guntle was terrified. She shifted into first and punched the accelerator to the floor. The tires spun but the car wouldn't budge. The ditch was too deep. She clawed at the gearshift, but the damned thing still wouldn't move. Tires whined, and it rocked from side to side.

Guntle couldn't breathe. She had to get out of that closed car. She pushed open the door, stumbled out into the darkness, and fled down the road. When she looked back, Guntle saw blue lights flashing in the distance.

After calling 911, Barry dialed her mother, Selma Guthrie, who lived nearby. While speaking on the phone, she could see the lights of the car outside. Barry knew that the station wagon was stuck in the drainage ditch beside her driveway, and that only a wrecker would be able to pull it out.

She heard the approaching sirens, and suddenly her driveway was filled with Kentucky State Police cruisers. Before the officers entered the house, she went from room to room, turning on every light in the house. Then she turned on the floodlights outside.

As an investigator took her statement, others began a meticulous search of the house. In a closet next to Barry's bedroom, they found her clothes riddled with bullet holes. Technicians dusted the entire house for fingerprints.

Amazingly, there was no blood inside the house. But on a patio door leading into the garage, officers located a shoeprint, later found to match one of Childress' shoes.

As Barry gave her statement, Kentucky State Police initiated a search of the grounds and surrounding area. The troopers had found massive amounts of blood in the old sedan. They concluded that the gunman couldn't get far.

Meanwhile, detectives traced the license plate. They found that the car belonged to Tonya Marie Guntle, of Bowling Green. They also determined that at least two men had broken into the house.

After forcing entry into the garage, the intruders had encountered a sturdy kitchen door with three locks. Unable to kick it in, they'd found a pick-ax in the garage and used it to smash through the door. They'd begun to loot Barry's house — they had gone so far as to place a teakwood jewelry box on her car.

Outside, as the troopers prowled the area with spotlights, they heard a voice calling from a field across the road. Someone was yelling for help. A state trooper moved cautiously toward the suspect. Lying on his stomach in the grass, he identified himself as James Shugart.

"Can't breathe," he gasped. "I need oxygen." Shugart lay in a pool of blood, his eyes fluttering in their sockets. "Some woman shot me," he said. "Oh God, I think I'm gonna die."

"Son," the trooper retorted as he snapped handcuffs on the wounded man, "in your line of work, it's called an occupational hazard."

Shugart's arrest record was extensive. He was known to local police as a professional burglar and drug addict. He was transported to a local hospital, where surgery saved his life. However, the bullet had blasted through his colon, causing permanent damage.

Guntle, Shugart's girlfriend, was quickly arrested. As was her custom, she had left her four young children home alone while she drove the getaway car.

A few days later, Childress was arrested.

Each suspect was charged with attempted murder and armed burglary. They were ultimately convicted and sentenced to long prison terms.

In a recent interview, KSP investigator Stan Harlow stated that he attempted to obtain a statement from Shugart while he was in the hospital recuperating from the gunshot wound. Although Shugart refused to speak with the detective about the bungled burglary, he wanted to talk about Ann Barry.

"That woman," he said, "was just looking to shoot someone."

As if it was the victim's fault, Harlow thought.

In a recent interview, Barry stated that the police treated her with the utmost respect. "My brother, Jim Guthrie, and his wife, Georgia, came to be with me that night," she remembers.

"The troopers were talking with Jim about his experiences in Vietnam, and one said, 'Hey, Jim, you should have had your sister with you when you were in Nam.' Jim replied, 'I sure could have used her.' Of course, they were just trying to make me feel calm and secure."

"We're living in violent times, and it is getting worse," Barry continued. "Littleton is one example. With population and economic pressures, along with the perennial threat of nuclear warfare, I cannot visualize any measures society can take to thwart the actions of mentally deranged minds, young and old."

Ann Barry received massive support from the community, and got national attention for her successful defense of her life. In addition to having her story heralded by national commentator Paul Harvey, she acted in a re-enactment for an Arts & Entertainment television special entitled, *Guns Under Fire*. Other radio and television interviews followed.

Barry spoke of her feelings on gun control. "I have no problem with raising the age of gun sales to 21," she said, "although young men and women fight our wars at 18. Many of these young people are angry that they can't privately own a handgun."

She continued, "Having sellers at gun shows to require background checks is okay. Safety locks are a good idea if you have children, but keep at least one gun hidden away — loaded and ready to use in case of an emergency. It should be well located, and in a place only the owner knows about, so you don't have to run all over the place to get to it.

"One suggestion has been to require combination safety locks. That's crazy! The gun is in the dark, unloaded, and you're trying to work a combination lock, load a gun, and be ready to protect your family from a home invasion, all within a matter of seconds. Forget it — you're dead, murdered by criminals who follow *no legal restrictions!"*

Barry cringed at the thought of what would have happened to her had she been required by law to have her gun secured with a safety lock. She knows she would be dead.

Chapter Four
The Last Ride
of 'Yo Roller

"I still carry concealed, which doesn't make going to work an event I look forward to each morning." Dennis Grehl, July 17, 2000.

The door opened, kicking a brief blast of frosty air into Redford Pharmacy. A young man entered, his sneakers tracking crusts of ice across the floor.

It was Saturday afternoon, January 18, 1997. Just another day in another Detroit ghetto.

Jennifer Knott stood at the counter. When the man had appeared at the door, she'd clicked a buzzer to allow him to enter.

Pharmacist Dennis Grehl was at the other end of the counter. He was talking on the telephone. Grehl had worked at the drug store for 35 years. In 1961, while still a teenager, he'd begun as a courier, delivering prescriptions to the store's customers. He later interrupted his employment to serve in the U.S. Army, then complete his degree at Ferris State University. In 1968 he came back to Redford to stay.

Grehl had seen the area change. What had once been a mixed-race, middle-class neighborhood in which residents waved and spoke to one another had become a menacing slum. Crack addicts and prostitutes openly hustled on the streets outside, and nearly every business on the block had been robbed at least once.

An experience that had occurred in 1990 had profoundly affected Grehl.

Dennis Grehl

He'd been robbed.

Because of this, Grehl had begun carrying a gun, a .32-caliber Beretta semiautomatic that he kept in a holster behind his back.

"I have a permit to carry a concealed handgun," he recently told the author. "[That's] not an easy thing to get in this area. But I had received formal firearms training in the military, so I was proficient with handguns."

The customer who had entered the store wore a green jacket and blue jeans. Knott noted that he appeared clean-cut, thin, and handsome. But when he stepped up to the counter, he snapped, "Gimme the money, bitch!"

At first, the clerk thought he was joking. She wasn't even nervous until the customer opened his jacket. There, tucked into his trousers, she saw the butt of a revolver.

Grehl was still on the phone. He hadn't noticed that the store was being robbed.

The robber motioned toward the cash register.

Knott tapped out the entry code. The cash drawer popped open and she began scooping out bills. Keeping her composure, Knott purposely let several flutter to the floor. She hoped Grehl would notice.

He did. The pharmacist glanced at her, but was still unaware that the man standing four feet away was anything other than a customer.

Then the bandit reached over the counter, snatched the money, and shouted, "I'll take that and a lot more, bitch!"

It suddenly hit Grehl like a flashback. We're being robbed again, he thought. He remembered the robbery in 1990 when he'd been forced to the floor by two gunmen. The amount of money they got, about $900, didn't matter. But the vulnerability he'd felt, the total loss of control, the fact that his life might end just so some crackhead could get another hit — he had been so enraged that he swore it would never happen again.

At that moment, the robber glanced at the pharmacist. For a moment, their eyes locked. It was then that Grehl determined to stop the man. He reached behind his back for his gun. At the same moment the robber reached for his own gun. It was like a quick-draw showdown straight out of Dodge City.

Grehl won. He yanked the .32 from his holster, raised his arm, and aimed. The robber's gun was in his hand and he was swinging it toward Grehl when the pharmacist fired. The crack of the gunshot echoed through the little store, followed by a surreal silence.

The robber slumped to the floor, kicked once or twice, then lay motionless. A stream of blood oozed down his face. The pharmacist's shot had struck the bandit in the middle of the forehead.

In the silence, the air smelled like gunpowder. The two store employees looked at each other, then glanced down again at the robber. The pharmacist wanted to retch. Then he placed his gun on the counter and waited as Knott called police.

Anthony Williams had been preparing for his own funeral all his life. He may not have known it, but his lifestyle dictated that he would die young.

He was one of seven children. Although the family lived in a housing project in Chicago, his mother worked hard to support the family.

Williams got into trouble early and often. At fourteen, he was suspected of murdering his best friend. But the police were unable to prove it, and the charges were eventually dropped. Two years later, he dropped out of school. Another year passed before he left Chicago a step ahead of the law. He moved from one ghetto to another, this one in Detroit.

Some women found him attractive, and he quickly learned how to charm them. He sired five children by three different women, and he always kept a few girlfriends on the side. But he never married any of them.

By seventeen, he was a full-fledged drug pusher. He had all the accoutrements of the trade: big cars, heavy gold chains, and women.

Williams went by the street name "'Yo Roller." To local gangs, the name meant "rolling to another heist."

Eventually, though, Williams fell prey to the drug dealers' trap — he began using the stuff he sold. He could handle marijuana, mescaline, even heroin, all staples of his business. But crack cocaine was another story. He quickly became addicted to the drug. Now the women could come and go, but a baggie was always his constant companion. At 36, Williams still had his looks and trim physique. But those who studied him closely could see the frantic eyes of a crackhead.

'Yo Roller was always armed. Unlike Grehl, however, he didn't bother to get a permit. And his gun dealer didn't have a license — Williams bought his guns on the street, or he stole them.

At least once a day, the crackhead put his gun in his pocket and hit the streets searching for another mark. But no matter how much he stole, there was never enough money to support his habit.

In 1986, Williams was arrested for illegal use of a firearm. The charges were later dropped. In 1988, cops stopped him for speeding and found seventeen packages of crack cocaine in his clothing. He pled guilty, but was given probation. In 1991, he was again arrested for possession, but he walked again.

As happens so many times with violent criminals, Williams would never serve a day in prison.

By the time he decided to rob Redford Pharmacy, 'Yo Roller had become a shadow on the dark streets. He came and went, making nightly trips to the crackhouse to pick up his next hit. His business had dried up, because now he smoked everything he could get. Each day he needed more, and still he couldn't get enough.

On that cold, snowy afternoon, Williams was desperate. He needed some blow, and he needed it quick. 'Yo Roller was prepared to murder someone to get it.

Police arrived within minutes after the shooting. They escorted Jennifer Knott and Grehl to the police station. Investigators questioned the employees for an hour, then released them.

On Monday, the Wayne County district attorney called Grehl to inform him that he wouldn't be charged. The shooting has been ruled a justifiable homicide.

In an interview, Grehl reflected on his feelings about the first robbery when he was forced to lie on the floor with a gun to his head. "That's a position you don't want to be in," he said. "It's absolute, complete helplessness. You're not sure if they're going to eliminate witnesses."

After the 1990 robbery, the company installed a buzzer system to screen customers before letting them come into the store. They also installed a panic button, and forbade employees from working alone. And in an unusual policy decision, the company owner authorized Grehl to carry a firearm on the premises.

Jennifer Knott credits Grehl with saving her life. "I thought my life was going to be over," she said.

"Flash — right in front of my own eyes."

In the last few years, Grehl has seen his neighborhood deteriorate even more. Now steel bars cover all windows and doors of the few businesses that remain. Employees no longer live in the area. Instead, they slink in from the suburbs, put in their eight hours, then flee, thankful to have survived another day.

Grehl plans to work for two more years, then retire to Florida.

He looks on what he did as something that was necessary. But it still haunts him. "I can't say I'm glad I did it," he said. "But I'm glad it didn't turn out the way it could have. To this date, I still don't always sleep well at night." He paused, then added, "But at least I survived."

Chapter Five
Home Intrusions

"In 1994, I was raped and I didn't have a weapon. I compare that with what happened this time." Michelle Ayres, May 24, 2000.

We like to think we're safe in our own homes. But home invasions are becoming more prevalent, the robbers relying on the element of surprise and terror to subdue homeowners. In many cases, the home invaders wear SWAT team uniforms, and use police-speak to momentarily confuse their victims. The invader knows a homeowner is less likely to shoot if he or she thinks the intruder is a police officer.

Unlike home invaders, burglars prefer stealth. But many are prepared to resort to violence should they unexpectedly find someone at home.

In other cases, such as in the attempted rape of Michelle Ayres, the thug was undoubtedly stalking his victim, waiting for her husband to leave.

The taking of property by force is not new, nor is it unusual to find homeowners fighting back.

In these stories, and in thousands of other cases in my files, the property owner was able to survive the attack of violent criminals only because he or she had a gun.

X

At 5:15 p.m., on December 26, 1998, Mary Lou Krause sat in the kitchen of her single-story, brick house in Swanton, Ohio. Her husband, Jerry, was cooking dinner. "It was fish," Mary Lou remembered.

Mary Lou Krause

She glanced up and saw someone move past the picture window. She told her husband that a person she didn't know was at the back door.

Mary Lou walked into the bedroom and retrieved her Astra .22-caliber revolver. Then she moved back into the kitchen and stood a few feet from the door, out of sight of the man on the porch.

The food on the stove was still sizzling.

The man at the door wore a dark coat that fell to his knees. He asked Jerry for directions to the local Masonic Lodge. This wasn't unusual — the Krause's lived near a major highway and people often stopped to ask for help if their cars broke down or if they needed directions. Jerry cracked the door and began explaining how to get to the Lodge.

In a recent interview, Mary Lou recalled, "The next thing I heard was a voice shouting, 'Let's all go inside!' This was a loud, booming voice. The next thing I seen was this arm coming through the door with a big gun." Suddenly, Jerry Krause was struggling for his very life.

Jerry Krause

A second man appeared. The two assailants began trying to force Jerry back into the kitchen. But the retired masonry foreman was having none of that. He fought back, and the battle became a give-and-take as the attackers attempted to push him inside while the homeowner used his shoulder to keep them out.

As the battle raged in the doorway, Mary Lou maneuvered herself so that she could shoot at the assailants without hitting her husband. The man with the gun saw her and simultaneously raised his pistol to fire.

Mary Lou recalled, "I stepped out from behind the door and fired. I hit him in the arm and he immediately returned fire. His bullet grazed my hip."

The assailants panicked and ran.

"As he got back out by the gate," Mary Lou said, "he turned around and fired again. [The bullet] hit the house and ricocheted into the screen door. But by that time I had slammed the big door shut."

Mary Lou and Jerry Krause got down on the floor and crawled to the kitchen. Jerry closed the drapes to cover the big window, then retrieved his own gun. While Jerry dialed 911, Mary Lou turned off the stove and stood guard at the window.

"It happened so fast you just had to go on instinct." Mary Lou said later. "When the first man knocked on the back door, the second man went around to the front of the house and tried to open the front door which we always keep locked. When he couldn't get in, he ran all the way back around the house and jumped on my husband's back, trying to help the first man. The two of them were trying to wrestle him through the back door."

Investigators arrived a few minutes later. They circled the house and called out the canine unit in an attempt to track down the suspects.

"The sheriff's department did an excellent job," Mary Lou recalled.

An ambulance transported her to the hospital where her flesh wound was treated and bandaged. She then returned home.

The next afternoon, a man with a gunshot wound appeared at a Toledo hospital. He was arrested and charged with aggravated assault and attempted first-degree murder. Christopher Mathews, the gunman, had been hit in the right shoulder. He later plea-bargained his sentence to five years in prison. With good behavior, he could be out in less than two.

Mary Lou states that she's incensed by the lenient sentence. "He tried to kill us," she said. "Another half-inch and I'd have been dead."

She credits a plan that she and her husband devised with saving their lives. She said, "We're almost seventy years old, our house is semi-isolated, so we have to take care of ourselves. The best way I know to do that is to have a gun and know how to use it.

"People need to have a self-protection plan. If I only save one life, it'll be worth it. When people knock on the door, I look out the picture window. If I know them, I let them in. If I don't know them, I get my gun and stand behind the door so they can't see me, and I let my husband talk to them. I'm ready if I'm needed.

"One day a woman came and asked to use the telephone. She never knew that while I was sitting there I had my gun under the newspaper. You can't be too careful.

"A handgun is a necessity for everybody. I wouldn't feel safe without one. The government shouldn't ban handguns."

Sheriff Jim Telb called Mary Lou Krause's actions heroic. "She was protecting her home," he said. "She was absolutely correct in defending herself and her husband."

Mary Lou has made only one change in her plan. Now, instead of a .22-caliber pistol, she has a .38 Special. "It makes bigger holes," she said.

II

On the morning of June 4, 1998, Michael Merz was in the upstairs office of his Boca Raton, Florida, home when he heard a thump at the front door. Merz lived in the upscale Isles of Palms subdivision, and had been at work on his computer.

At first, he thought the noise was made by a UPS deliveryman dropping off a package. Then he heard a loud crash. He suddenly realized that someone was trying to break in.

Merz, who owns several firearms, had recently moved them downstairs so he could clean them. In a recent interview, he said, "When I knew someone was breaking in, I walked down the hall to the bedroom. I began going through the chest of drawers looking for a gun, because I thought I might have left one up there."

The homeowner's adrenalin was pumping, but he managed to remain quiet as he searched for one of his guns. When he couldn't find one, he began to walk downstairs.

"I didn't think the guy was in the house at that point," Merz said. "I thought, I've got time to go downstairs and get my gun from the kitchen. It was a Sig-Sauer P230 .38-caliber."

As Merz started down the stairs, he saw the intruder coming out of the downstairs bedroom holding a cordless telephone. Both men looked at each other in surprise. Then the intruder bolted for the front door.

Merz didn't hesitate. He dove off the stairs and tackled the man. They fell into the kitchen, then wrestled into the garage.

In the violent struggle, two of Merz's motorcycles were knocked to the floor.

Merz recalled, "In the few minutes that I was looking for the gun, he had already staked out the downstairs. He had unlocked the door leading into the garage so that he had another means of escape and had already put my car keys in his pocket. What he was going to do was load my car up and leave with as much as he could steal."

Now the struggle became desperate. As they rolled across the floor, the intruder grabbed Merz by the throat. The homeowner slipped the hold, and landed on top of the intruder. "He was almost as big as me, so I couldn't manhandle him," Merz recalled. "But I could sort of dictate which way the fight went."

Merz wanted to get the intruder back into the house so he couldn't escape. Capture him, thought Merz. This man needed to be in jail. He was obviously an experienced burglar, and maybe more than just a burglar.

As they fought back into the kitchen, Merz remembered the gun he'd hidden in the cupboard above the stove. At this time, however, he was unable to get to it. The two men fought back into the living room. At one point, Merz was on his back, and the intruder had one hand around his throat while he balanced the other hand on the floor. This gave Merz the opportunity to get both hands around the throat of the intruder.

"I was squeezing with everything I had," Merz said. "We fought back into the kitchen. By this time I'd had my hands around his throat for a long time and we were both pretty exhausted. I knew it was going to take a few minutes for him to recuperate, so I jumped up and grabbed my gun."

Merz leveled the barrel between the man's eyes. "His eyes got big as saucers," Merz said. "He went from being aggressive and violent to completely submissive. He couldn't have been more cooperative. He wouldn't even look at me. He just looked down."

The homeowner reached for the telephone and dialed 911 while still holding his gun on the burglar. When he told the dispatcher he'd captured a burglar in his home, she told Merz to order the man to put his hands on the back of his head.

Merz went her one better. "Lay face down and put your hands behind your back!" he ordered. The man quickly complied.

The operator asked Merz to find out the name of the intruder. The homeowner reached into the man's back pocket and retrieved a billfold. It was obviously stolen. The driver's license photograph was that of a middle-aged man — the intruder was in his early twenties.

"What's your name?"

The intruder was so frightened of the gun that he told the truth. "Michael Ratliff," he said. After a few moments, the dispatcher informed Merz that the man had two warrants out for his arrest.

Police arrived quickly. While searching the burglar, they found a knife in his pocket. This allowed them to charge him with armed robbery. Ratliff's long arrest record consisted of convictions for burglary, drug possession, grand theft, assault, and trafficking in stolen property. A few minutes before breaking into Merz's house, he had attempted to break into the home of a woman who lived in the same neighborhood.

Ratliff was eventually sentenced to four-and-a-half years in prison. The sentence was mandatory, and there is no chance of parole.

Merz, who had used a handgun to frighten away a burglar several years before, feels that the Second Amendment gives individual citizens the right to own firearms. "To me it's mind-boggling that people would want to take guns from law-abiding citizens."

❚❚❚

Ninety-one-year-old Sebron Mitchell had outlived his wife, children, and most of his friends. The former chef lived alone, subsisting on Social Security and a small pension. His house, in what he referred to as a "rough" section of Augusta, Georgia, was a four-room, clapboard shack. "It may not be much," he always said with a smile. "But it's home."

On three previous occasions, his house had been burglarized. So Mitchell bought a gun for protection, an H & R .32-caliber revolver.

A few minutes before midnight, on February 4, 1999, Mitchell was about to go to bed. Suddenly, there was a thundering crash at his back door. Then he heard footsteps rushing toward him.

"It was a few moments of sheer terror," he later recalled. "The man literally tore the door down. The door just fell apart."

It looked to Mitchell like a scene out of some old black-and-white, B-grade movie. When the door plunged down, clouds of dust, thick as smoke, poured into the room. A stranger appeared out of the dust, brandishing a hunting knife.

Mitchell had no time to react. The intruder rushed the homeowner. He grabbed Mitchell and began choking him. The former chef couldn't breathe. He tried to struggle but was no match against the younger man.

"I need money!" the man said.

"I'll give you money," Mitchell croaked.

It was like the assailant never heard him. As he continued to choke Mitchell, the intruder pressed the knife against the homeowner's side. The blade drew blood.

"You wanna die, old man?"

Mitchell wanted to respond, but his assailant had cut off the air from his windpipe.

Suddenly, the intruder released his hold. Mitchell gasped for air. "I'll give you money," he repeated.

Again the man ignored Mitchell's offer. He again tightened his grip on the homeowner's throat, this time applying excruciating pressure. The attacker leveraged his body so that the homeowner fell. Mitchell's leg kicked a rickety table, knocking it to the floor. A glass on the table shattered. The intruder fell on top of Mitchell, choking him and continuing to keep the knife pressed against his side. By now, blood had soaked the homeowner's shirt.

Mitchell couldn't breathe. He knew he was going to die. At least, he thought, I've lived a full life. If I die now, I'll go to a better place. A strong Christian, he thought of his friends at the Mt. Zion Missionary Baptist Church he attended.

Again, the man released Mitchell. This time he stood up. Looking down at the homeowner, he screamed, "Man, I need some cash!"

Mitchell tried to speak, but his voice box wouldn't work.

"Gimme money, old man!" the intruder said, lacing his commands with violent obscenities. "You better gimme some cash!"

For the first time, Mitchell looked into his assailant's eyes. What he saw frightened him — the lost, spaced-out eyes of a drug addict. The former chef had seen it before. One of the restaurants he'd worked for in Augusta had hired several probationers as cooks — one of them was a "dope fiend," as Mitchell recalled. His eyes had the same look as the intruder's.

The homeowner finally regained his voice. "Quit choking me and let's go find some money," he said.

Mitchell pulled himself up and led the intruder into the kitchen. After the last burglary of his home, he'd stashed his gun there. Now he was determined to get to it.

In the kitchen, he pointed to a drawer that contained several dollars in rolled coins, change that Mitchell allowed to accumulate until he could take it to the bank to exchange it for bills.

The intruder pulled open the drawer. The weight of the coins caused the drawer to fall to the floor. Several of the rolls burst, spilling pennies, dimes, nickels, and quarters all over the floor. Mitchell's assailant seemed mesmerized by the hundreds of coins. He fell to his knees and began trying to replace the coins in the torn rolls.

This gave Mitchell the opportunity he needed. He opened a drawer, pulled his pistol, and pointed it at the intruder. "Everybody had told me if they break in my house again, then shoot to kill," he recalled. "Well, I did. That dope fiend took one bullet but he didn't take a penny of my money." Mitchell aimed his revolver at the assailant and fired twice.

He watched the intruder fall. Blood pooled on the floor around the man, and he began to crawl away. Mitchell held the gun on him.

"Stop!"

But the man ignored him. The intruder jumped up, ran through the house, and scampered out the back door.

Mitchell breathed a sigh of relief, then picked up the telephone and called police.

Sergeant Greg Smith responded to the call. He found Willie James Hall lying on the ground outside Mitchell's house. The robber was in obvious pain, and stammered that he'd been shot. Smith examined the man and discovered that one of

Mitchell's bullets had hit the assailant in the right leg. A deputy administered first aid.

While waiting for paramedics to respond, Smith called in Hall's name for a background check. The results didn't surprise the officer. Hall's rap sheet listed more than twenty years of arrests in Georgia.

The crack addict was taken to the Medical College of Georgia Hospital and treated. Later, he was released to the custody of the police and placed in jail.

Hall was convicted on charges of burglary, criminal attempt at armed robbery, and possession of a knife during the commission of a crime.

A shaken Mitchell told police, "It just wasn't my time to die."

IV

On May 1, 2000, Michelle Ayres was fast asleep. It was 1:00 a.m. in the peaceful community known as The Colony, Texas, a town near Plano.

"I heard a thump out in the living room," Ayres recalled. "My daughter sleeps out there."

Her year-old twin sons slept in an adjoining bedroom.

Ayres, who had been awake for almost forty-eight hours taking care of her sick children, figured her two-year-old daughter had brushed against the wall, and would call for her mother if she needed anything. When the toddler didn't call, she drifted back to sleep.

The housewife recalled, "I suddenly woke up to this excruciating pain in my face and my ribs. A man was on me, his legs straddling me, and he was beating me in the face and the ribs."

Pinned beneath the weight of a two-hundred-pound assailant, the shock of the attack momentarily paralyzed her. Then Ayres thought of her children. She began to struggle against the man.

He growled, "Gimme what I want and I'll stop hitting you." Memories of having once been raped came to her. This only made Ayres more determined to fight.

In the pitch darkness, the struggle seemed to go on forever. The more she resisted, the more he punched her.

"Lay still, bitch, or I'll kill you!"

Ayres thought of her husband, Chris. He was working but she knew he always kept a loaded pistol beneath his pillow for protection. She determined to try to get to it.

The housewife pushed against her assailant and caught another punch to the ribs. It took her breath away. Then she felt her nose explode. She knew the intruder had broken it.

With her left hand, Ayres reached beneath her husband's pillow. At first she couldn't find the gun. She nearly panicked. Her only means of staying alive was so close, yet so far away.

Then the desperate mother lunged toward the weapon and suddenly felt the cold steel on her fingers. Ayres pulled it out, a .45-caliber Colt MklV Series 80 semiautomatic pistol. She was familiar with the gun. Before they'd had children, Chris had taken her to the shooting range many times.

She recalled, "I believe [the intruder] felt me reaching for the gun, because all of a sudden he grabbed my wrist. He held it really tight and I almost dropped the gun. That's pretty scary. The safety was on, but I was able to release it with my thumb."

With a twisting motion, Ayres freed her wrist from the assailant's grip. Swinging the gun toward him, she squeezed the trigger. Ayres heard the explosion and saw the muzzle flash.

"A few seconds later," she recalled, "I felt the bed move. Then he was gone. I have a cordless phone next to me, and I picked it up and dialed 911."

The police arrived and called for an ambulance. Ayres' fractured nose was gushing blood. Her lip was split, her eyes were blackened, and her ribs bruised. Ayres said, "The nightgown I was wearing was all torn up. The bed sheet was a bloody mess, as well as my pillow."

Police called Chris at work. The concerned husband raced to the hospital to be with his wife. While it was comforting to know that his firearm had saved her life, one look at Michelle tore her husband apart. Chris later stated that if he could have gotten his hands on her attacker, he would have killed him.

Investigators determined that a window near the back door had been broken, and the intruder reached through it to unlock the deadbolt and the doorknob. He then ransacked the kitchen, finding Ayres' billfold.

She later recalled, "My wallet was open on the counter and he had taken my credit cards and insurance papers. The kitchen drawers were open. In the living room, my CDs were scattered everywhere, and my stereo was knocked over. The police think he wore gloves, because there were smudges all over the house. But there were no fingerprints."

Investigators believe the assailant was watching Michelle before he broke in, possibly stalking her from a distance. He knew when her husband left for work, and he had watched the lights go out when she went to bed.

Police could not determine if the intruder was hit. The 230-grain Hydra-Shok jacketed hollow-point bullet that Ayres fired struck the master bathroom doorjamb and ricocheted along a wall before coming to rest.

Investigators tested the bloody sheets and other items in the house, but, as of this writing, the assailant hasn't been caught.

"Police have told me off the record," Ayres said, "that if I hadn't had my husband's gun, I probably would have been murdered, and my children may have been killed, too.

"I'm against gun control because if you put a gun on a table and don't touch it, it's not going to get up by itself and shoot someone.

"When I woke up and this man was punching me, I was extremely scared, but I made up my mind I was not going to be a victim again. Then I thought about my children, and I got angry."

Ayres paused for a moment, then continued. Pain welled up inside her, and tears formed in her eyes.

"In 1994," she said, "I was raped. I didn't have a weapon, and I compare that with what happened this time. I feel a lot safer with a gun."

Michelle Ayres now has her own pistol. It rests beneath her pillow.

Chapter Six
The Squeeze-cocker

"Some people say I was lucky. Possibly. But the fact that I had fired thousands of rounds in practice was one factor in saving my life." Joseph Montgomery, March 12, 1999.

Joseph Montgomery

At 10:00 a.m., on September 3, 1998, Joseph Montgomery had just opened for business. The 56-year-old owner of *500 Guns*, located near the Indianapolis Speedway, watched as two men entered the store. They walked up to a row of glass cases and began browsing.

Both men wore casual slacks and conservative shirts. Their hair was cut short and they seemed well-mannered. Montgomery later recalled, "They dressed normal and acted normal, and that is why I was taken by surprise."

One of the men pointed to a firearm and asked to examine it.

Montgomery left his desk near the rear of the shop and walked behind the case. Pulling out the Intratec TEC-9 that the man had pointed to, he handed it over.

"How much does it cost?" the man asked. Montgomery noticed he was soft-spoken and articulate.

The shop owner told him the price and explained that Indiana required a five-day waiting period for a firearm purchase. The man said he understood. After handling the gun for a few minutes, he handed it to the second man, who then gave it back to Montgomery.

"I need to go get some money," the first man said.

"There's an ATM just down the block. I'll be back for the gun later."

Montgomery placed the pistol back in the glass case and watched the two men walk out the door.

Each morning, he mentally checked several places in his store where he had hidden loaded guns. In case of an emergency, the gun shop owner wanted to have a weapon available. This morning was no exception — Montgomery glanced at the areas where he'd stashed his "protection" guns.

Lining the walls of the shop were deer antlers, stuffed ducks, even a wild turkey. All were trophies from Montgomery's favorite hobby — hunting. During the fall of each year, Montgomery and his son made it a point to take time out for several hunting trips.

Chapter Six
The Squeeze-cocker

He looked over his shop once more. Several stools were spaced in front of the display case, and a cash register sat on a counter near his desk.

The shop owner reached into the pants holster behind his back and examined the Heckler & Koch P7 he always carried. This little gun wasn't much bigger than a .380-caliber, but it packed the wallop of a 9mm. Through wire-framed glasses, Montgomery examined it, making sure the magazine was full.

He always kept a round in the chamber, because a safety feature unique to the P7 made it difficult to fire unless the shooter knew how to operate it. The shooter must squeeze the grip with his firing hand to depress a "squeeze-lever" built into the front strap of the grip-frame. Only then would the gun fire when the trigger was pulled.

After assuring himself that the gun was in working order, Montgomery soon had other customers. He forgot about the two who'd left to go the ATM machine.

After an hour, his customers were gone and the businessman was alone again.

At about 11:45 a.m., Montgomery heard the front door open. The two men who had left for the ATM machine walked back in.

"We've got the cash now," one of them said.

Montgomery followed them to the counter. This time the man pointed to a different pistol, one on the bottom of the shelf.

Montgomery still didn't suspect the men had anything on their minds except purchasing a handgun. "I bent down to get the gun out of the case," he recalled, "and when I came up, one of them grabbed me around the neck. The other one stuck a 9mm Ruger to my forehead."

The man with the gun shouted, "This is a stickup. We're taking all your guns, man!"

Montgomery struggled to free himself, but the man who was holding him had a grip like a vise. Both assailants stood more than six feet tall with hard, bulging muscles.

"We gonna kill you, man!"

Montgomery noticed that now they were using street language, peppered with obscenities.

"Shoot him!"

The shop owner reached behind his back for the P7, but the assailant who was choking him grabbed his hand. They struggled for the weapon, and Montgomery felt his thumb being twisted back. He grunted in pain as the thumb snapped. Events were moving from bad to worse. Now one of the robbers had taken the P7.

"Down on the floor, man! *NOW!*" shrieked one of the men. The gunman with the 9mm slammed it against Montgomery's temple, knocking his glasses to the floor.

Montgomery instantly decided that he was not going to lie helpless on the floor — at least, not voluntarily. He later recalled, "I had seen too many horrible video clips of robbers who, after they push somebody to the floor, they start shooting them while they're laying face down. I figured at this point, I'm dead already, so why should I lay down and let them shoot me in the back of the head?"

The robbers kept glancing at the plate glass windows. If a customer walks in, thought Montgomery, they'll kill him. It was obvious the gunmen had planned to quickly dispose of the shop owner. They hadn't anticipated that he would fight back.

Unable to push their victim to the floor, the robbers began shoving him toward the back of the store. The man holding his neck pulled out a knife and pressed it against Montgomery's throat.

Before the robber could slash his throat, Montgomery grabbed the blade. He felt it slice into his hand. Then he winced as he saw his blood spill to the floor. The three men struggled past the storage room and into the office area. There the assailants slammed Montgomery against his desk, showering the floor with papers. Together they continued to shove the struggling shop owner toward the rear of the store.

"Shoot him!"

With a final heave, the robbers threw Montgomery to the bathroom floor. The man holding Montgomery's P7 trained it on him while the second robber moved toward the surveillance camera situated high on the wall near the front door. As he attempted to remove the tape from the camera, he screamed, *"Do him in the bathroom! Do him now!"*

Montgomery recalled, "After the first robber pushed me into the bathroom, he was trying to figure out how to use the P7, which is the main reason I carry it. He was squeezing the cocking lever, which is in the front on the grip, and he tried it two or three times. But he couldn't figure out how to shoot me with my own gun."

The robber glanced out the door at his partner. In that split second, he sealed his own doom.

Montgomery had hidden a gun in the vanity underneath the sink. It was a .357 Magnum Smith & Wesson revolver, and it had been placed there for that very purpose.

The distracted robber shook the P7 as if he was trying to rattle it. The shop owner wrenched open the vanity and pulled out his gun. The robber looked down at him, his eyes widening. Montgomery aimed and pulled the trigger. CLICK!

Oh Jesus! he thought, my gun's misfired.

Hope filled the robber's eyes as he again leveled the P7 at the shop owner.

The second time he squeezed the trigger, Montgomery's Smith & Wesson boomed.

The robber screamed, then slammed against the wall. Just like in the movies, thought Montgomery. Then he cranked off two more rounds. The robber slumped to the floor beside Montgomery's desk, hit three times in the chest. He lay on the floor, his body jerking.

Now the storeowner became the stalker. He stood up, composed himself, then moved out of the bathroom. A bookcase, holding dozens of reference books about guns, sat against the wall, and the store owner used it as a shield.

Glancing out toward the floor of his shop, he saw the second robber stuffing his pants full of guns. The man had at least a dozen pistols in his waistband. The guy thinks his partner killed me, Montgomery thought.

As the storeowner stepped out from behind the bookcase, the robber's face twisted in amazement.

This guy's supposed to be dead.

The robber dropped behind a counter and pointed his gun at the storeowner.

Montgomery fired first. The shock of the concussion made his ears ring.

The robber stood straight up, aiming his gun at the storeowner.

Montgomery fired again.

The assailant suddenly collapsed to the floor. The second shot hit him in the forehead, driving through his skull and tearing a baseball-sized hole in the back of his head. Finally, the place was silent.

Montgomery thought of his wife and son. He'd managed to survive, and now he said a silent prayer.

For a moment, he stared in shock at the gruesome scene. Blood was pooling on the floor beneath the second robber — splatters even spotted the walls and plate glass window.

Finally, Montgomery staggered to the phone and called 911. The dispatcher told him to stay on the line until the paramedics arrived. "You don't need an ambulance, and you don't need paramedics," Montgomery said. "They're both dead. Just get the police here."

The first officer to arrive at the scene found both men lying dead. One was slumped behind Montgomery's desk, and the other lay on the sales floor near the window. Both had guns stuffed into their pockets and belts.

It didn't take the police long to identify the men. They also learned that both men had long criminal records.

The robber behind Montgomery's desk, Jimmy Smith[*], 24, had been repeatedly convicted for possession of cocaine and robbery. When he attempted to rob Montgomery, Smith was wanted for violation of probation.

The second robber, Daniel Walford[*], 23, had convictions for robbery, vehicle theft, various drug charges, and resisting arrest. A few weeks before, he'd been sentenced to serve 545 days in the county jail for armed robbery and vehicle theft, but that sentence had been suspended.

Montgomery was treated by paramedics for his injuries. He was not charged with any crime. Indianapolis Police Department spokesman Tim Horty said, "It appears that this is a pretty classic self-defense case."

In a recent interview, Montgomery stated, "If you're going to carry a gun, you'd better be proficient at using it. Even at the range I had to shoot the second robber, it was about 25 yards. He was half-hidden beneath the counter, so all I had as a target was his head and shoulders.

---

[*] The names of the perpetrators have been changed.

"On a monthly or bi-monthly basis, my son and I go to the range and practice some of these scenarios. Quick-draw stuff, like pull and fire in a panic situation to save your life. It'll really wake you up as far as finding out which guns you're able to shoot proficiently."

He spoke of the German-made P7 he used to thwart the robbers. "It's a semiautomatic 9mm," he said. "You squeeze the front of the grip to cock the gun. Then it's ready to fire. As long as you keep squeezing, it will keep on firing, but the minute you release it, it's de-cocked and won't fire. It's a very safe gun to carry, but I carried it for the reason that most people can't figure it out if they're not familiar with it.

"There was another robbery here a few years back. The owner had a .45-caliber Model 1911 semiautomatic, and it was basically the same scenario. They tried to shoot him with his own gun, but it was cocked and locked and they couldn't figure out how to get the safety off. So he was able to get another gun and survive the attack. It was shortly after that I started carrying the squeeze-cocker."

Montgomery explained that the Heckler & Koch P7 is a very uncommon weapon with unique features. The lever is initially very stiff to a person who doesn't realize it is there, and it feels just like part of the handle. Black-on-black, the lever is not immediately noticeable to most people who pick it up. The first time someone attempts to shoot the gun, the lever feels just like part of the handle and the shooter doesn't know to squeeze it.

"In this country," Montgomery said, "there are already 22,000 laws controlling the sale of firearms and ammunition. But after the horrible tragedy in Littleton, Colorado, the politicians are trying to pass more gun control legislation.

Chapter Six
The Squeeze-cocker

"The real truth is that the blame [for Littleton] really lies with our liberal society, where you can't punish anybody for anything, and no one is responsible for his own actions. So they try to blame an inanimate object, such as a hammer or knife or gun.

"When you're dealing with government and politics, truth and logic don't enter into the picture.

"Every year, you've got two-and-a-half million people who save lives because a firearm was available to them. But the politicians and media never mention that."

On September 3, 1998, Joseph Montgomery was among those who saved his life because he had a firearm.

Chapter Seven
Concealed Carry

"If one of us hadn't hit him, he might have turned around and emptied that shotgun into the dining area." Robert Guerry, September 22, 1997.

On September 22, 1997, O.R. "Ryland" Moore and his wife, Margaret, were enjoying the "Early Bird Special" at Sam's St. Johns Seafood at 4453 Blanding Boulevard in Jacksonville, Florida.

Moore, who had a permit to carry a concealed weapon, usually took along a Star PD .45 ACP caliber semiautomatic pistol. But because of the late-summer heat wave, Moore decided to carry a lighter North American Arms .22 Magnum 5-shot single-action revolver. He'd dropped the small gun into his right hip pocket before going out.

It was about 7:15 p.m., and more than thirty patrons were crowded into the small restaurant.

A few feet away, Birmingham, Alabama, resident Robert Guerry was having dinner with his daughter. Guerry, also a concealed permit holder, never left home without his .22 Magnum derringer.

The clink of glasses and whispers of conversation created a relaxed atmosphere for the diners.

Suddenly, Moore heard the manager yell, "We're being robbed!"

Moore looked up and saw a man dressed in camouflage burst through the front door. The robber wore a hood over his head and held a sawed-off pump-action shotgun. The stock had been cut off to form a pistol grip.

"Everybody down!" the robber screamed. "On the floor! On the floor!"

He swung the shotgun toward the dining area. Moore noticed the man's finger was on the trigger — a slight squeeze and the gun would fire. Moore knew that a sawed-off shotgun loaded with buckshot could kill or wound dozens of people if fired in a crowd. He was determined to stop this man.

The patrons of the restaurant began diving beneath their tables, while employees also dropped to the floor as ordered.

A preparation area stood in the middle of the restaurant. As soon as the robber entered, several waitresses ducked behind the wooden counter, trying to slide out of sight. The robber saw them and ran to the counter. Grabbing waitress Amy Norton by the arm, he forced the frightened woman to her feet. The gunman then pulled her to the cash register. He seemed to have tunnel vision, his eyes focused only on Norton. He didn't notice Moore or Guerry when they stood up.

Moore reached in his pocket and pulled his gun.

"Ryland!" his wife whispered.

He didn't know if she was encouraging him or trying to get him to cooperate with the robber. However, he noticed that she didn't duck to the floor.

Norton had been working at the restaurant for only a few days. She was still unfamiliar with the cash register.

The gunman waved the shotgun in front of her face. "Open it now or you're gonna die," he said.

The frightened waitress punched the keyboard, but in her panic, she hit multiple keys and jammed the machine.

"Open it, bitch!"

The robber's angry tone made her believe she would be killed. He held Norton with his left hand — the shotgun was in his right hand. When she was unable to open the register, the robber stuck the barrel against her temple.

Moore had read recent newspaper accounts of mass shootings in restaurants. Helpless employees and customers had been murdered by trigger-happy thugs. He could visualize the same thing happening here.

The robber was growing panicky. "Open the box or I'll kill you," he screamed.

It's now or never, thought Moore.

Unexpectedly, Norton pushed away and ducked beneath the register.

This gave Moore the opportunity he was looking for. In a recent interview, he stated, "My plan was to aim at body mass (shoulders to groin, left arm to right arm, rib cage to rib cage). Being a competitive shooter for forty years, I knew the limitations of the gun. For that reason, I didn't want to risk a head shot."

Moore aimed and fired.

Almost immediately, he heard a second shot echo from his right side.

Guerry had also fired at the robber.

At the sound of the shots, the robber turned and sprinted across the restaurant floor to the front door. Before he reached the door, he began to limp. Moore knew that at least one of the shots had found its mark.

The gunman, now obviously disoriented, held the shotgun diagonally across his body. As he approached the door, the barrel slammed against the doorframe, then clattered to the floor. The robber left it where it lay as he fled.

Moore recalled, "I watched [him] run out the door and along the length of the building to my left. The whole wall of glass was all the way to the end of the building. After he disappeared from my view, I went to see if he was gone. As I walked outside, I noticed the shotgun between the double doors on the floor, minus the pistol grip. I looked and saw the grip about 40-50 feet away in the parking lot. By this time, a lady in the restaurant was calling the police on her cell phone."

After making sure the gunman was no longer in the area, Moore went back into the restaurant and saw many of the customers still lying on the floor. He announced that the robbery was over.

Patrons began to pop up from beneath the tables.

By this time, police began to arrive. Blue lights whirled against nearby businesses, and a crowd gathered outside.

The first officer took the guns from Moore and Guerry. After questioning everyone in the restaurant, the two were informed that they had acted legally and would not be charged.

An officer, listening to a hand-held radio, confided in Moore, "The robber was just admitted to the emergency room." Then he winked and said, "Gut shot."

Moore went back to his meal, which was now cold. As he walked toward his table, he was met by each patron of the restaurant, as well as the manager and employees, who stood in line to shake his hand.

His wife was beaming. Moore asked her why she hadn't gotten down on the floor like the others. "I knew you'd handle it," she said.

A shaken Amy Norton later credited Moore and Guerry with saving her life.

Dervonne Marquise Moore (no relation to Ryland Moore) was admitted to St. Vincent's Medical Center suffering from a gunshot wound. Detectives G.H. Strickland, L.B. Williams,

F.L. Christmas, and E.J. Martin were dispatched to the medical center.

They learned that Moore was a 17-year-old student at Ed White High School. Doctors confirmed that the suspect had a bullet wound to the left side of his lower abdomen. The detectives determined that the wound would be consistent with that of the robber at Sam's St. Johns Seafood Restaurant.

However, the bullet was near vital organs so it could not be removed. Therefore, it couldn't be tested to determine who actually fired the bullet that had struck the robber. Although police later concluded it was likely that Ryland Moore's bullet was the one that had hit the suspect, they could not be sure.

In his initial statement to detectives, the suspect stated that he was driving by Nathan Bedford Forrest High School when a group of "guys" began yelling at him. After an exchange of words, someone pulled a gun and shot him. A friend had driven him to the hospital.

When Detective Christmas informed Moore that he didn't believe him, the suspect clammed up.

A few minutes later, Moore's mother entered the room. It was obvious to the detectives that the woman took pride in herself. She was well-dressed, composed, and articulate.

After speaking with the detectives, she glared at her son and said, "You *will* tell the officers the truth."

A sobbing Moore then made a second statement. He related to detectives that a friend, Lawrence Allen, had provided the shotgun and the getaway vehicle. Moore's job was to go into the restaurant and rob it while Allen stayed in the car as the lookout.

When he was shot, Moore ran outside and jumped into the car. As they fled from the scene, Allen cursed him for bungling the robbery and dropping the shotgun. Police could easily identify them, said Allen, because Moore's fingerprints were all over the gun. His accomplice threatened to take Moore "out in the woods and bury" him. Finally, the wounded robber persuaded the angry Allen to drive him to the hospital.

Moore was arrested, and placed under armed guard until he recuperated enough to be transferred to the juvenile detention center. Lawrence Allen was also tracked down and arrested.

In a recent interview, Ryland Moore said, "My entire motive was to separate the perpetrator from his firearm."

Unfortunately, not everyone applauded his actions. A column in the *Florida Times Union* by Amir Abdul Rashid was typical. "Last week's shooting," he wrote, "raises important questions about the old line between being a concerned citizen getting involved and being a vigilante... I believe Moore and Guerry crossed that line."

In a written response, Moore stated, "For your information, we have a standard which we call *laws,* which stipulates [that] a person may use deadly force when his or her life is threatened. If this is blurry, perhaps you need to study up on what exactly is a concerned citizen and what exactly is a vigilante."

The overwhelming response to the shooting, however, was acclaim. Moore was interviewed on local television stations and was a guest on more than a dozen radio talk shows. An avid proponent of concealed-carry laws, he was able to educate many people about the purpose and legality of concealed carry.

By any measurable standard, the "shall issue" concealed-carry laws passed by nearly thirty states in the 1980s and 1990s have been extremely successful. (These statutes allow law-abiding citizens who meet certain criteria to carry concealed weapons.) In fact, Florida's concealed-carry law may be the most successful piece of legislation ever enacted in that state.

Passed in 1987, it quickly became a model for other states. The law mandated that permits to carry concealed weapons would be issued to any Floridian who passed a background check and successfully completed a course in gun safety. (Before the "shall issue" laws were passed, local law enforcement officials had discretionary powers to issue or not issue permits. In many counties and states, *no* permits were ever issued, regardless of need.)

Between October 1998 and January 1999, Florida issued 551,000 permits. Only 109 were revoked because the licensee used a firearm in the commission of a crime. In other words, the success rate was 99.999%.

By contrast, the dropout rate for Florida's high school students is approaching 50%.

If the two were graded, Florida's concealed-carry law would grade out as an A+ while its high schools would rate an F-.

Other states report similar results. Virginia passed concealed carry in 1995, and out of more than 50,000 permits, by 1999 not one licensee had been convicted of a firearms-related crime. Between 1994 and 1998, Arizona issued 63,000 permits — only 50 were revoked.

Kentucky passed its concealed-weapons law in 1996. By 1999, more than 51,000 citizens had obtained licenses. According to an investigative feature published in the *Cincinnati Enquirer* on August 20, 1999, State Representative Bob Damron, a Democrat who sponsored the law, stated that he "wasn't aware of any case in which charges have been filed against a concealed-carry permit holder." On the other hand, the newspaper described several cases in which Kentuckians with concealed-carry permits had acted in self-defense to stop a crime.

One of the reasons concealed-carry laws are so successful is that they are designed to aid law-abiding citizens who feel a need for protection from violent crime. During an 8-year period from 1987 to 1995, the state of Florida received only 723 applications from convicted felons — and most of those had had their citizenship reinstated.

When Ryland Moore and Robert Guerry pulled their guns and shot Dervonne Moore, it was in the tradition that concealed carry has established: law-abiding citizens using firearms to stop violent crimes.

Unfortunately, in this case, Florida's criminal justice system failed again. The robbers of Sam's St. Johns Seafood were given mere slaps on the wrists. Dervonne Moore was sentenced to 12 months in the county jail. Lawrence Allen plea-bargained down to 50 hours of community service.

Each year, thousands of concealed-carry permit holders use their guns to stop criminal acts. Here are a few examples:

Willie J. Redding should have been in jail when he attacked two Wal-Mart employees in Spring Hill, Florida. On May 23, 2000, he appeared in court on shoplifting charges. Because of a long criminal history that included eleven previous felony convictions, prosecutors argued that bail be placed at $60,000. But Hernando County Judge Peyton Hyslop, known for his lenient sentences, ignored their request and lowered the bail to $3,000.

Redding was back out on the streets that afternoon.

A few hours later, he walked into Wal-Mart and attempted to steal a VCR. When he was confronted by two employees, Redding dropped the appliance and pulled out a knife. He began slashing at the employees.

"Drop the knife! Drop the knife," someone screamed.

During the melee, both employees were cut.

Sandra Suter, standing in the checkout line, heard the altercation. Pulling a .40-caliber semiautomatic pistol from her purse, she rushed forward to help the beleaguered employees.

"I have a concealed-weapons permit," she shouted, as she stuck the gun between the assailant's eyes. "Either drop the knife or I'll kill you!"

Redding dropped his weapon and meekly surrendered to the grandmother.

A spokeswoman for the Hernando Sheriff's Department stated that Suter acted "responsibly," and would not be charged.

On June 16, 2000, Jan Moskow was walking home in the pouring rain from the Philadelphia bakery he owned. He wore a raincoat, and a yarmulke to cover his head. Hearing footsteps behind him, the baker turned and found a man pointing a gun at him. Moskow raised his hands as instructed by his assailant.

The robber shouted, "Give me the money!"

"Okay," Moskow responded.

Reaching into a pocket as if to retrieve money, the baker instead pulled a 9mm semiautomatic pistol. He fired twice, and the assailant slumped to the sidewalk in a pool of blood.

Raheem Stewart was hit once in the forehead. He died at the scene.

Moskow, who has a permit to carry a concealed weapon, was cleared. According to District Attorney Joseph LaBar, the shooting was an "exceptionally clear [case of] justifiable homicide."

On December 23, 1999, Paul Carr had just parked in front of his Houston, Texas, convenience store. As he got out of his car, a late-model Chevrolet Suburban pulled in behind, blocking his vehicle. Two armed men jumped out of the Suburban and rushed toward Carr.

When they were about ten feet away, one of the assailants began shooting at Carr. The business owner quickly pulled his own licensed handgun and returned fire.

A full-scale gun battle suddenly erupted on the normally quiet street. One of the robbers fell, but got up and ran back to the Suburban, followed by his accomplice.

Police quickly responded. A few blocks away they found the robbers' vehicle, which had been stolen. Inside, Alberdeen Williams lay dead of gunshot wounds.

A few minutes later, Lavar Butler was admitted to Memorial Northwest Hospital. Doctors stated that he had a bullet wound to the side. After recovering, Butler was charged with attempted murder and aggravated robbery. He was also charged with being a "persistent felon."

Paul Carr was not charged.

On June 20, 2000, the *Philadelphia Inquirer* reported that one of two men who tried to carjack a motorist had been shot and killed.

Before confronting the unidentified motorist, Deshawn Norwood and an accomplice had unsuccessfully attempted to rob several men who were gambling on a nearby street corner. When they resisted, Norwood shot one of the men in the thigh, then fled.

A few minutes later, he and his partner tried to steal the car of a 26-year-old who was stopped at a traffic light on Fishers Lane. When the motorist refused to get out of his car, the pair shot at him. The driver then pulled his own licensed handgun and fired at the men.

One of the unidentified motorist's shots hit Norwood in the chest, killing him.

Police said that the driver acted lawfully, and would not be charged.

On April 29, 1998, in Tulsa, Oklahoma, Donnie Neal Moore, a mental patient, became embroiled in a dispute with his landlord at the apartment complex where he lived. An enraged Moore ran outside. Spying an elderly woman walking toward the apartments, he ran to her and yanked a heart monitor from her waist. The assailant smashed the monitor on the asphalt, then knocked the woman's walker out of her hands. She collapsed on the ground.

Gene Case was landscaping the grounds of the apartment complex when he saw Moore's attack on the elderly woman. When he yelled at the man to leave her alone, Moore raced up to Case and began screaming obscenities at him. The landscaper, who had a permit for concealed carry in Oklahoma, ran to his truck and pulled out his .45-caliber semiautomatic pistol.

By this time, the disturbed man took off running across the parking lot. When he saw a mother getting out of her car holding a two-year-old child, he approached her. Suddenly, without warning, Moore snatched the baby from the arms of its mother.

Somebody yelled, "He's stealing that woman's baby!"

Case ran after the fleeing man and finally caught up with him near the edge of the parking lot. Training his handgun on the assailant, Case ordered him to place the baby on the ground. Moore, looking down the barrel of the gun, did so.

"Please don't shoot me," he begged.

The child's mother, who had joined the chase, ran up, grabbed her baby, and carried it to safety.

Case, still holding his gun on the man, ordered him to get down on the ground. Moore pulled his pants and underwear down below his knees and sat down.

An obviously deranged Donnie Neal Moore was later committed to a psychiatric hospital.

Police applauded Case for the restraint he used in not shooting Moore.

Chapter Eight
Break and Enter

"He's a good robber, but he ain't no Boy Scout!" Richard Arlen Hibdon's accomplice, referring to Hibdon's inability to tie a knot.

Wilma Roberts awoke at 3:17 a.m. "Teddy Bear" and "Teco," her two Chihuahuas, were barking furiously.

The retired nurse, a widow for 34 years, lived alone in her Spanaway, Washington, home and slept in an upstairs bedroom.

It was June 7, 1995.

Roberts, wearing a nightgown, got out of bed and crept to the bedroom door. Peering down the hall, she noticed that someone had turned on a light downstairs.

Before she could react, she saw a man rushing toward her.

Roberts turned to retreat to her bedroom, but her assailant grabbed her from behind. She screamed, and he clamped a hand over her mouth. Roberts tried to jerk away, but the man held her so that she was unable to move. She later recalled, "My heart started beating. He just enveloped me. He gripped me so tight. Then I saw another man."

As the homeowner continued to struggle, her assailant placed a gun to her head. The steel barrel against her temple frightened the woman so much that she stopped fighting.

"Get in the bedroom!" the gunman commanded.

Roberts hesitated.

"NOW!"

When she didn't move fast enough, her assailant punched her face. Stars danced in front of her eyes, and she thought she would pass out. The only thing that kept her conscious was the blood she felt dripping down her cheek. The gunman forced a wobbly Roberts into the bedroom and flung her onto the bed.

"Pull the covers over your face," he ordered.

Again, the homeowner did not move fast enough. The assailant picked up a heavy quilt and threw it over her head.

In the darkness, she heard him rifling through her chest of drawers. Roberts kept a .38-caliber revolver beneath her bed, and resolved to try and get it.

Then she heard the robber move to the closet. Roberts had also stored a .22-caliber revolver on the shelf in there. She prayed that the intruder wouldn't find it.

After what seemed like an hour, she heard him leave the bedroom. As he moved down the stairs, Roberts reached under the bed, her fingers searching for her gun.

"What ya looking for?"

Roberts jumped at his voice. The assailant lifted the cover off her head. He looked angry.

"What the hell's going on?"

He again stuck the barrel of his gun to her head. Oh God, Roberts thought. I'm dead.

"I'm looking for my telephone," she lied.

Someone in the distance shouted, "Tie her up, Dick!"

The robber cursed, then jerked the quilt off of her. Roberts saw that her once immaculate room was a mess. Her clothes were piled on the floor, and a jewelry box had been emptied. Costume jewelry was scattered across the room. Even her shoes where strewn about the floor.

The assailant removed a shoe from the clutter on the floor. He unlaced the shoe, then grabbed Roberts' left arm and tied her wrist to the bedpost. He tightened the knot until it hurt.

Searching through her clothes, "Dick" found a cloth belt. He moved back to the bed and tied the homeowner's right wrist to the other bedpost. Now she lay face-up, spread-eagled across the bed.

When she looked up, she saw the intruder leering at her. Half of his lower teeth were missing. Roberts shivered at the thought that this monster might rape her. Teddy Bear and Teco would be no protection. They were whimpering in the corner.

Once again, the assailant began rummaging through her belongings. In a drawer, he found several cartridges.

"You got a gun?" he asked.

"No, my son took it," Roberts lied.

"Hey, bitch, if I find a gun, you're dead."

From the look in his eyes, Roberts concluded that he planned to kill her.

"Where are your bank cards?"

Roberts pointed to her purse lying on a chest of drawers. The robber pulled several credit cards from her purse, then threw it on the floor.

"Gimme a number."

Roberts told him the PIN numbers. The assailant found a pen and wrote down the numbers.

"How much you got in the bank?"

"You can only withdraw three hundred dollars at a time," Roberts said. She quickly realized she'd made a mistake. She'd heard of burglars killing their victims and withdrawing money day after day until the account ran dry.

The robber finally ended his search. As he walked out the door, Roberts saw that he held a plastic bag filled with her belongings.

Now that she was sure that he'd gone, she began struggling against her restraints. The shoestring was tight, and cut her wrist when she pulled at it. But the belt was loose. If she could get her right hand free, she might be able to untie the shoestring and get to her gun.

Roberts could hear the robbers laughing and talking downstairs. It was obvious that they were taking their time as they ransacked her house — she reasoned that they planned to spend the night stealing anything of value that they could carry. Then they would murder the only witness to their crimes.

Dawn was beginning to seep through the blinds when she heard her van start up. It was in the garage and she assumed they were stealing it.

Roberts believed she had only a few minutes left to live.

The struggle against the belt binding her right arm was beginning to pay off. The knot had loosened, and with a final pull, she jerked free.

It took her a minute, but she untied the string on her left wrist. Then Roberts dropped to the floor. She frantically fumbled around on the floor beneath her bed trying to locate the gun she'd hidden there. But it seemed that tons of clothes and debris had spilled beneath the bed.

Unable to locate the pistol among the clutter, Roberts got up and tiptoed to the closet. She held her breath, hoping the robber hadn't found the second gun she'd stashed there. On a shelf, she located it, an H & R Model 666 .22-caliber revolver. Breathing a sigh of relief, the homeowner quickly checked it to make sure it was loaded.

Now the former nurse moved out into the hallway. Peering out, she saw empty boxes scattered down the hall. It angered her to see that the robbers had shown no respect for her possessions.

As she turned toward the stairs, Roberts saw one of the thugs walking up the steps. She didn't hesitate. She aimed the gun and fired twice. The muzzle flashes lit the house, and the crack of the shots echoed in the semi-darkness.

She heard the robber scream and watched him tumble down the stairs. He landed on his back, but quickly jumped up and bolted back through the kitchen. She knew he was headed toward the garage.

Roberts descended the stairs, carefully scanning the room below. The second invader was nowhere to be seen.

On the floor beneath the bottom step she saw a smear of blood. Good, she thought, I hit him.

By now, Roberts had noticed that the robber was no longer the arrogant bully who'd tied her to the bed. In his panic to get to the van, he'd run headlong into her Harley Davidson motorcycle, knocking it over. Finally, he'd scrambled to the 1988 Chevrolet Astro van and jumped into the driver's side.

Roberts moved toward the garage. When she spotted the robber inside her van, she aimed again and fired. A window shattered, and the thud of a bullet ripped into metal.

The robber's face was contorted in fear as he stared at the women bent on avenging herself. He backed out of the garage, tires smoking.

Roberts followed and fired three more times.

Then the van disappeared into the pre-dawn darkness.

The homeowner took a deep breath and walked back inside her house. She still hadn't seen the second man. She didn't know where he'd gone, but she hoped he was no longer in the house. A shaky Roberts went to the telephone in the kitchen to call 911. It chilled her to find that the line was dead!

She walked back into the garage, got into her second car, and drove to a 7-Eleven convenience store down the street. There she called police.

Pierce County Sheriff's Department Detective Ed Knutson was assigned to the case. He was at Roberts' house organizing a forensics investigation when an anonymous call came into dispatchers at the station. The caller, a female, stated that a friend of hers had dug a bullet out of the arm of a man named Richard Arlon Hibdon. When the caller asked how he'd been shot, Hibdon stated that he was burglarizing a woman's home when she'd shot him.

Knutson was familiar with the suspect. The 21-year-old crack addict had a long history of arrests — in fact, Pierce County deputies sometimes joked that he was a "serial burglar."

The caller stated that Hibdon was recuperating from his wound at the Sahara Tan Salon in Spanaway. Knutson led a team of officers to the business and arrested the suspect.

Hibdon was then taken to the hospital for treatment. Doctors said the bullet had penetrated his right wrist, traveled up his forearm, and lodged in the elbow. The bullet had been surgically removed by a paramedic who was a friend of the suspect. The wound was nasty and very painful.

The suspect was taken to the hospital where his arm was treated and stitched. Hibdon was then transported to the sheriff's department for questioning. He voluntarily consented to give a statement.

The burglar said that he had no job, no car, and no residence. He was addicted to crack cocaine, needing a fix at least once a day. He lived on the streets, or at the homes of "friends" and acquaintances when they would let him. Hibdon stated that he supported his drug habit by burglarizing at least one house a day. Whatever goods he obtained were sold or traded to his crack dealer.

Hibdon confessed to burglarizing Wilma Roberts' home with an accomplice named Earnest James Lineberry. He stated that they'd gained entrance by breaking a window on the ground floor. Once inside, they heard the dogs barking. Hibdon had gone upstairs, found Roberts awake, and had forced her onto her bed. Once she was tied up, he and Lineberry had systematically looted the house of anything they thought they could sell.

Investigators obtained permission from Hibdon's girlfriend to search her house. They located three duffel bags filled with stolen property from Roberts' house. Inside the bag were small items such as jewelry, rare coins, pocket knives, cameras, and kitchen utensils. Also found were three television sets, a VCR, a vacuum cleaner, and $305 in cash. Other items were more unusual for burglars to steal. An electric grill, a chain saw, a mechanic's set of 86 tools, a CB radio, a hydraulic jack, and seat covers were discovered in the bags.

"Looks like he wanted to take a couple days off," one of the detectives joked.

The following day, Hibdon led officers on a "show and tell" of places he'd burglarized in recent weeks. Knutson was amazed. After locating twenty-six residences, Hibdon began having trouble remembering how to get to the other places he'd burglarized. Detectives estimated that the "serial burglar" may have broken into at least fifty homes within the last two months.

One telling incident had taken place two weeks before the attack on Wilma Roberts. Hibdon had broken into the home of an elderly woman. When she refused to give him her wedding band, he threatened to "cut off her finger" to get it. Eventually, Hibdon had used soap to remove the tight-fitting ring from her finger. The woman told detectives that she had been in fear for her life.

When Knutson asked Hibdon why he was going back upstairs after burglarizing Roberts' home, the suspect stated, "I was just gonna check on her."

Knutson didn't believe him. Why would he need to check on his victim if he and his accomplice had already completed their burglary and were in the process of leaving? Since Hibdon was carrying a gun, many of the detectives working the case felt that he was going back up to murder the woman who could identify him. What convinced them was that Hibdon knew she'd heard Lineberry call him "Dick."

Hibdon was later convicted of two counts of first-degree armed robbery and two counts of burglary. He was sentenced to ten years in prison.

Roberts later stated that she was glad she had her pistol handy. "If innocent people aren't armed," she said, "you can be sure the crooks will be. I've got a message. Honest people shouldn't turn in their guns. They'll only end up in the crooks' hands."

Chapter Nine
Shootout at the
"Stop and Rob"

"If no store merchants had guns, it would be open season on those [convenience] stores." Oakland County, Michigan, Sheriff Johannes Spreen, March 18, 1980.

Snow blanketed the ground outside the three-store plaza. A bitter wind ripped in from the north, frosting the breath of the man who stood beside an old Pontiac sedan. The car was idling, blowing black smoke from its exhaust. Two men sat in the front seat, nursing the last of their cigarettes. They'd rather have been toking but had no money for pot. They watched as the last customer left Richardson's Farm Dairy, a convenience store situated in the plaza.

It was Saturday, 10:30 p.m., March 15, 1980, in Clarkston, Michigan. The store was getting ready to close. Two clerks were on duty: Darlene Ramsey, and night supervisor Charmaine Klaus.

Ramsey, a pretty 21-year-old part-time college student, was working her last weekend at the store. On Monday, she was to begin a new job in the medical field with a physician. It had long been her dream to become a medical technician.

Klaus sat in the back office, counting receipts. In her desk, she kept a loaded .38-caliber Smith & Wesson Chief's Special revolver. It was against company policy, but Klaus' husband, U.S. Army Sgt. William F. Klaus, had insisted she bring it. A recent rash of convenience store robberies in the area had culminated in several clerks being kidnapped, tortured, and murdered. In fact, it was getting so bad that local cops had begun staking out selected stores in isolated areas.

Outside the store, the man beside the Pontiac pulled on a green ski mask. He checked his gun, a Colt semiautomatic pistol chambered to fire the .38 Super cartridge. Nodding to his companions, he moved toward the store.

Charmaine Klaus

In a recent interview, Klaus recalled, "I left Darlene with twenty dollars in change and took the rest [of the cash] to make out a bank deposit. I went through a narrow back room and into an eight-by-eight-foot office." The room had no windows, but it did have a door in the back that staff kept locked.

Before she could begin her bookkeeping chores, Klaus heard a commotion outside her door. She recalled, "Darlene came running in my office and said, 'There's a masked man with a gun out there.' I told her to lock the door and I reached for the phone to dial 911. I had my hand on the phone getting ready to call the police when he started shooting through the door." Splinters flew everywhere.

Ramsey stood paralyzed. Somehow, though, the first fusillade missed her.

Still sitting at her desk, Klaus was unable to believe this was happening.

The robber, using his shoulder, crashed against the door. After three tries, it banged open. Ramsey was thrown against the far wall. As the clerk stood wide-eyed, the man raised his gun and shot her twice. Ramsey, her eyes wide in disbelief, crumpled to the floor.

Klaus remembered, "I knew I didn't have time to call anyone, so I reached into my drawer on the side of the desk and pulled out my revolver. [The robber] pointed his gun in my direction. All I could see was his mask. There were two holes for the eyes and a hole for the mouth."

Instinctively, Klaus aimed at his face. She pressed the trigger, and the .38 barked.

The gunman jumped back out into the hallway so that she could no longer see him.

Ramsey began to crawl across the floor, trailing blood like a wounded animal. She ended up behind her supervisor's chair, as if seeking protection.

Abruptly, the robber reappeared. He opened up again, showering bullets in every direction. Klaus was unable to get off a second shot. The torrent of gunfire forced her to dive beneath the desk.

She recalled, "Bullets kept flying around my head so I crawled underneath the desk, which was the worst thing I could have done. He came into the room, and it was so small that his body blocked me so I couldn't move. Then he pulled Darlene up by her hair. I heard her say, 'Oh, Char...,' and that's the last thing she ever said. He shot her once in the head." The gunman dropped Darlene to the floor.

When he turned toward Klaus, she saw that the round she'd fired had struck home. Blood was pouring out of his mouth, soaking his mask and his shirt.

He pointed the gun at Klaus's head. She remembered, "When something like this is happening, it's in slow motion, and a lot of thoughts go through your head. I remember thinking; thank God I shot him because now if he kills both of us, they'll know who did it — they'll have evidence because my bullet is in him. That's all I could think of, along with the knowledge that I couldn't [position myself to] shoot him again because his body was blocking me."

The gunman surveyed his trapped victim. Klaus, squeezed beneath the desk, had her gun pinned underneath her. The robber raised his pistol and suddenly fired again. The bullet blasted into the desk.

"When he shot through the desk, it sounded like a roaring train," Klaus recalled. "I put my hand up to my jaw and ear, like a natural reaction to the sound. That's what saved my life. His bullet went through my hand and into my jaw, then into my trachea. But the bullet had broken up in my hand and that's what saved my life. He tried to shoot again but the gun was empty. Finally, he turned and walked out through the back door."

Klaus waited until he was gone, then crawled over to Darlene. She determined that her co-worker was still breathing, but the breaths were coming in slow gasps. Klaus cradled Ramsey's head for a moment, then got up and walked to the back door.

When she looked out to make sure the robber had left the area, she saw a bloody trough in the snow. The robber must have fallen, she thought. Good, he must be badly wounded.

After determining that the gunman was gone, Klaus closed the door and locked it. Moving deliberately, swaying back and forth and using the walls for support, Klaus walked toward the front of the store.

She stared in amazement! Several customers were standing at the counter with items to be purchased. They began to berate Klaus because no one was there to wait on them. One man threatened to never shop at the store again.

"I was holding my hand over my face. I guess the blood wasn't gushing out, so they didn't know I was shot. When I told them, they began to panic, to just go crazy!"

Finally, a customer calmed down long enough to call police.

When the robber had fled out the back door, the store's security alarm had sounded. But instead of calling the police, representatives of the alarm company phoned Klaus's husband and began complaining about the alarm going off so often.

Sgt. Klaus immediately took charge. "It's not closing time yet," he said. "So you better get an ambulance and police on the way." Finally, the representative relented and called 911.

Charmaine Klaus remained conscious throughout the ordeal. She saw the first police cars arrive, followed by ambulances with spinning red lights. After police cleared the scene, paramedics placed the women on stretchers and transported them to the hospital.

Ramsey, who had been hit in the head, abdomen, and forearm, was rushed to Pontiac Osteopathic Hospital. She was pronounced dead at 12:45 a.m. Sunday morning. Klaus was transferred to Pontiac General Hospital. According to a report by her physician, Dr. John Alter, the gunshot "passed through her hand shattering several bones in her hand and entered the left side of her face, also causing a comminuted compound fracture of the mandible on the left side. The projectile was then deflected downward into the neck, fracturing the larynx, creating severe upper airway obstruction which required immediate surgery... for a tracheotomy and exploration of the larynx."

It would take five years and numerous surgeries before the store manager completely recovered from her wounds.

Investigators discovered large splotches of blood in the snow outside the store, indicating that the robber had been severely wounded. It was also obvious that he had fallen twice, and that someone had picked him up and transported him from the scene.

Officers contacted local hospitals and asked them to be on the lookout for a man with a gunshot wound.

A few hours later, Albert Joseph Hartford, 22, was admitted to Detroit General Hospital with a gunshot wound to the mouth. Oakland County detectives were contacted, and Hartford was arrested. Doctors stated that the only reason he survived was that the bullet had hit a tooth and split in two. One piece stuck in his cheek, while the other lodged in the robber's throat.

The gunman's brother, Charles, 17, and Michael Gosciki, also 17, were later arrested as accomplices. The local press demanded to know why they were being charged with murder when they hadn't pulled the trigger. Oakland County Prosecutor L. Brooks Patterson said, "They did more than just sit there. They drove the vehicle. They drove Hartford to the hospital. They were more than just spectators."

All three had previous arrests and convictions. In fact, Albert Hartford was due to face charges for several drug offenses and part of their purpose in robbing the store was to get money to pay his lawyer. They had robbed two other stores that morning.

On September 5, 1980, Albert and Charles Hartford went on trial together for first-degree murder.

The presiding judge was one of the most notorious jurists in the country. Judge William J. Beer, in addition to siring three children with his wife, also had nine children by his mistress.

Beer was known throughout the state for his liberal sentencing. Once when a defendant was convicted of rape, Beer allowed him to remain free to see if he could "straighten up his life."

Klaus recently recalled her impressions of the trial. "[Albert Hartford] was convicted," she said, "because of my testimony, [because of] the bullet that was dug out of his throat, and [because] his blood was on the floor. I could never have identified him because he was wearing a mask. At the trial, he was dressed so nice, in a three-piece suit, with short hair, and my husband asked, 'Is that one of the lawyers?' He even grew a mustache to cover the hole in his lip."

Before sentencing, Albert Hartford claimed he was innocent. "I do not feel I was given due process," he said.

Referring to the ages of those sitting on the jury, he stated, "I'm not middle-aged. My peers are 18 to 25, not 35 to 45."

As happened so many times in Beers' court, his brother Charles was acquitted.

Judge Beers' behavior during and after the trial ignited Charmaine Klaus. She recalled, "I'm thankful that Michigan has a sentence of life in prison without parole for first-degree murder because of liberal judges like Beer. After the jury rendered the verdict of first-degree murder, Judge Beer apologized to the parents of Hartford, stating, 'My hands are tied, I must sentence him to life in prison.' Beer said this while Darlene's parents were still in the courtroom. Their daughter was dead and the judge apologized about having to send her murderer to prison for life."

Gosciki was later convicted of second-degree murder and served a mere two years in prison before being released.

Since that day in 1980, Charmaine Klaus has become a victim's advocate and a gun rights spokesperson.

She has appeared on numerous occasions before state and national legislators to push for right-to-carry laws. Her efforts paid off twenty years later when Michigan legislators adopted a shall-issue concealed-carry law.

Over the years, Klaus has been a guest on many radio and television shows, including the Phil Donahue show. She is a staunch defender of the Second Amendment and feels strongly that law-abiding citizens should have the right to bear arms.

Recalling her long medical ordeal, Klaus stated, "I was in intensive care for about two weeks, then hospitalized for two more weeks after that. I went through another five years of reconstructive surgery where they had to replace the bone in my jaw, and replace my teeth, and they did reconstructive surgery on my face."

Speaking of Darlene Ramsey, Klaus said, "It's a very sad story. She'd just turned twenty-one. This was going to be her last weekend at the store, because she'd just landed a job with a phlebotomist. She was very excited about it. That night ended her dreams of ever getting married, or having a family, or working in the job she really wanted. It just ended. Hartford just put the gun to her head and killed her for no reason.

"Emotionally, I think I'm better off than most victims because I had a chance to do something about my situation. There was some closure because of what I did. The perpetrator is in jail and he won't get out. A lot of victims don't find closure because they keep thinking, what if I did this, or what if I did that? I felt like I did the best I could in that situation, and we got some kind of closure out of it."

Things haven't changed much since 1980. Convenience store clerks are still the victims of choice for robbers, thieves, murderers, kidnappers, and perverts. The isolation of many of the stores, as well as the late-night hours, make clerks prime targets. Drop boxes for cash receipts, video surveillance cameras, and bulletproof bubbles haven't helped.

On the morning of May 27, 1999, Americans were stunned to turn on their televisions and see a videotape of a kidnapping in progress. Katie Poirier, of Moose Lake, Minnesota, was the clerk of a convenience store when she was abducted by Donald Blom. The clerk was forced from the store by an armed Blom, the scene captured on videotape by the store's cameras.

The abduction struck a chord in the American people. A 19-year-old girl working alone being forced to go with her kidnapper — it could happen to anyone's wife or sister or daughter.

Donald Blom was eventually arrested and confessed to taking the pretty clerk home, and raping and torturing her. Then he murdered her, dismembered her body, and cremated her. After Blom was arrested, it turned out that he had a long history of sex offenses. He was eventually convicted of first-degree murder and sentenced to life in prison.

It turned out that Poirer was a sitting duck. Because she was a teenager, she could not own a handgun. Because of the policies of the convenience store in which she worked, she was not allowed to be armed. Yet the store was located off busy I-35, giving the abductor the edge he needed to escape. Indeed, had it not been for the videotape, he might never have been caught.

Contrast that case with the following ones:

On January 27, 2001, at 5:20 p.m., Xiao Ming Lin was working the counter of Lin's Supermarket in Savannah, Georgia. His son was helping out and was also behind the counter. According to the *Savannah Morning News*, Johnny Tyson entered the store and pulled on a mask. He rushed to the counter and struck Lin with a brick, knocking the storeowner to the floor. Lin's son grabbed a handgun and shot the assailant four times. Tyson died at the scene. After a thorough investigation, the shooting was ruled justifiable homicide.

On February 1, 2001, the manager of the Spenard Motel in Anchorage, Alaska, was alone at 3:30 a.m. when a masked man rushed in waving a gun. John Yun handed him the cash drawer, but it wasn't enough. The robber pointed the gun at Yun's head. "He said he was going to kill me," Yun said when interviewed by the *Alaska Daily News*. The motel manager pulled a .38-caliber pistol from his vest pocket and shot the robber twice. The man fell to the floor, then raised his gun and attempted to point it at Yun. The manager fired several more shots, hitting the robber in the arm, leg, and face. The gunman survived, and Yun was not charged with any crime.

After five convenience store clerks were murdered in a five-day period, Houston clerks began arming themselves. Just one day later, on February 25, 2000, Khoa Nguyen and his sister, Huong Thi-Kim Nguyen, were behind the counter of their combination Texaco gas station and supermarket when two men entered. One of the men, Albert Gaston, jumped over the counter, grabbed fifty dollars from the cash register, then began to pistol whip Huong Thi-Kim. According to the *Houston Chronicle*, Khoa Nguyen shouted to the men, "You got the money. Now go." Instead, the two men began to beat Khoa. Then Gaston went to the front and locked the doors. At that point, Khoa thought they were going to kill the clerks and grabbed a handgun from beneath the counter. "We were face-to-face," he said. "He pointed his gun at me. I pointed my gun at him. I told him, 'Just run away. I don't want to shoot you.'" But Gaston kept coming. Khoa emptied his gun at the man, hitting him twice. Khoa then unlocked the door, allowing the wounded man and his partner to escape. Police quickly rounded up the wounded Gaston and his partner. Khoa was not charged. "I would be surprised if you find a store [in Houston] without a gun," he said. Authorities said the storeowner was within his rights to defend himself and his sister.

A Jacksonville, Florida, store owner turned the tables on an armed robber on February 15, 2001. Doran Moore entered the Holiday Grocery wearing a mask and carrying a handgun. But the owner saw him approaching and pulled his own gun from his jacket. Before Moore could shoot, the business owner fired, hitting him in the leg. The robber turned and ran. He later showed up at Shands Hospital, where police arrested him.

The storeowner, who did not wish to be identified, was found to have acted in self-defense.

On October 10, 2000, the *New York Daily News* reported that Meng Chin, owner of Joe's Cardville was behind the counter at 11:45 a.m. when James Baylor entered the store. According to the article, Baylor pointed a "Tech-9 submachine gun at Chen and demanded cash." Instead, Chen opened fire with his licensed Glock 9mm semiautomatic handgun. Baylor was hit four times and fell to the floor in a pool of blood. He was taken to the hospital and later arrested. Chen was "one-hundred-percent legitimate," said a detective. He was not charged.

On March 3, 2000, a man wearing a bandana over his face entered Hampshire Food Store and attempted to rob Getachew Alemayehu, an immigrant from Ethiopia, and his wife. When the man pointed a shotgun at Alemayehu, the owner dove to the floor, grabbed his gun, and fired three times. The robber staggered out the door and collapsed. He died at the scene. The storeowner was not charged, but was so upset at having to shoot someone that he was considering closing his store.

On February 10, 2001, the *Dallas Morning News* reported that a liquor store clerk had shot and killed an armed robber. Lisa Liev had been robbed a month earlier and still wore a bandage on her head from where she'd been beaten. During the second robbery, the assailant entered Johnny's Cut Rate Liquor Store at about 1 p.m. Sgt. Ross Salverino explained what happened. "When the robber attempted to shoot her, [Liev] fell to the ground," he said. "As the robber attempted to jump the counter, she got her weapon and shot the suspect once." After the shooting, Liev ran outside and locked the door so the robber couldn't leave. She then called 911. The robber died at the scene. Liev was not charged.

And so it goes. Day after day, Americans use firearms to survive violent attacks. Store clerks, homeowners, students, octogenarians, males, females, the disabled — a gun is the equalizer.

Chapter Ten
Armed and
Dangerous

"A shotgun will beat a pistol every time." Unidentified investigator for the Florida Department of Law Enforcement, December 14, 1999.

Many readers of my previous book have asked me how I find cases of armed self-defense. After reading news reports of a case that interests me, I contact the local law enforcement agency that investigated the case and ask for police reports of the incident. Once I receive the reports, I contact the victim who fought back and request an interview. I then try to obtain additional documentary evidence, such as court records, statements from investigating officers, etc.

Readers may be interested in reading the police report of an actual case, with only minor editing for clarity. Below is the nearly verbatim report of a self-defense shooting from the Florida Department of Law Enforcement. The report was acquired through Florida's open record law. It is public record, and may be published.

This incident occurred in rural Lafayette County.

"On Tuesday December 14, 1999 at approximately 2230 hours [Special Agent] B. Mortenson was contacted by the Lafayette County Sheriff's Office in regards to the shooting and possible homicide of a wanted fugitive identified as Brian Keith Franklin (W[hite]/M[ale] 7-30-65).

"SA Mortenson responded to the area of CR 420 and US 27 in Lafayette County and met Deputy Sheriff W. Savy. Deputy Savy advised SA Mortenson that earlier he had responded to the area of [County Road] 420 and the Maypop Cemetery where a suspicious van had been reported.

"Upon arrival at approximately 2103 hours, Savy met with Christopher Mullins (W/M 3-15-61) who he recognized as being from the Lafayette County area and another W/M with red hair, later identified as Lindsey Gary Lay (W/M 6-6-79). The two subjects were attempting to fix a flat tire on a Plymouth Voyager Van bearing a Florida tag, CK582B. Lay gave Savy a fictitious name as well as several different stories about where he was from and the ownership of the van. When Savy learned that the van was stolen he attempted to arrest Lay. Lay fled on foot into the surrounding woods while Mullins stayed by the van. Mullins told Savy that he had been assisting in getting the tire fixed and he was not involved with the occupants of the van in any other fashion.

"Deputy Savy had the K-9 unit from the Mayo Correctional Institution respond and they began tracking Lay. The search began approximately 2130 hours and continued into the early morning hours of Wednesday December 15, 1999. The Department of Corrections dog handlers were identified as Lt. Clark Hendrick, [and] Sgt.'s Mike Calhoun and Jeff Walker.

"During the search at approximately 2205 hours the Lafayette County Sheriff's Office received a call from the Raymond Driver residence requesting a deputy respond to the shooting of a suspect who had tried to break into the home. Deputy Savy reported that he had heard a muffled sound he believed to be the shot fired at the intruder at the Driver residence. Since it was so muffled, he was not sure where it was coming from and did not realize that it was from the

Driver residence which was only a quarter of a mile from the cemetery and search area.

"SA Mortenson proceeded to the Driver residence where the Lafayette County EMS unit was present. The paramedics were working on a subject later identified as Brian Keith Franklin. The EMS personnel present were paramedics Bobby English and Trevor Hicks, volunteer Regina McCray, and EMS Supervisor John Bell. The suspect Franklin was lying in an area just north of the residence/garage area and appeared to have multiple wounds to his upper left chest and neck area. The sheriff's office radio logs indicated that the EMS unit arrived at the scene at 2228 hours and began working on Franklin to assist his breathing and stop his loss of blood. (Note: The radio logs for the above date and times will be placed in the related items section of the case file.)

"The EMS unit had been requested at 2215 hours and had arrived at the scene at 2228 hours. They worked on the suspect until 2315 hours during which time they had been in contact with Shands of Live Oak Emergency Room Doctor Nasrullah, and at that time the suspect was pronounced dead due to lack of life signs and internal bleeding.

"SA Mortenson met with Sheriff D. Walker and Deputies A. Newell and Brian Lamb. D[eputy]S[heriff] Lamb briefed SA Mortenson on the scene as of that time. SA R. McDaniel arrived and assisted SA Mortenson and Deputy J. Young in processing the crime scene. SA McDaniel took digital photographs of the crime scene and these will be placed in the related items section of the case file.

"While SA McDaniel and Deputy Young were videotaping and photographing the scene, SA B. Mortenson interviewed the residents of the house, Helen and Raymond Driver.

"Helen Driver gave SA Mortenson the following account of the events leading up to the shooting. She stated that she had been watching the Dolly Parton Christmas special on Lifetime Television and her husband had just gone into the bedroom to go to bed.

"She heard the screen door on the back porch squeak and got up to see who was on the porch. Her mother-in-law resides next door to her house and she thought at first it was her coming over.

"She looked on the porch and did not see anyone at first. She went into the laundry room and turned on the porch lights and walked back into the dining room and saw a W/M standing on the porch. She cracked the glass sliding doors in the dining room and asked him what he wanted. He told her he needed or wanted to use her telephone.

"As the suspect was talking to her she saw a pistol in his right hand which he was holding down by his right leg. She immediately slammed the door and locked it, calling to her husband at the same time.

"As she shut the sliding door the suspect walked to the north end of the porch and broke out the glass part of the laundry room door/window. Once he had done this he was able to reach his hand into the room and unlock the door.

"Mrs. Driver called 911 after she shut the door and called again to her husband. As she was waiting for the 911 [dispatchers] to answer she saw the suspect come into the doorway between the kitchen and the laundry room. As he came into sight she saw him raise his pistol and heard her husband fire his shotgun. The shot struck the suspect and he began walking towards the living room. He turned and went back outside the house by the same door he had entered. She did not see or hear from him after he left the house.

"Raymond Robert Driver gave SA Mortenson the following account of what he saw and did that evening. He stated that he had just gone into his bedroom, which is adjacent to the living room and dining room. He heard some noise coming from the porch and got out of bed. About that time, he heard his wife say 'no' and heard her shut the sliding glass door between the dining room and the screen porch. He heard her call him and he got his 12-gauge shotgun off the gun rack in his bedroom. The weapon was loaded with three rounds of #1 buckshot.

"He heard the glass breaking in the laundry room door and as he [came] into the dining room from the bedroom he saw the suspect come into the doorway between the laundry room and kitchen. As the suspect pointed the pistol at him, Mr. Driver fired his shotgun striking the suspect.

"The suspect began walking in the laundry room towards the living room and was heard to moan 'oh no' or something like that. The suspect turned and went back out the door he entered and walked away from the residence.

"Mr. Driver turned his Sears 12-gauge model 200 pump shotgun, serial number 26388, over to SA Mortenson who later turned it over to DS J. Young. SA Mortenson also confiscated one fired 12-gauge shell and two loaded shells. Both of these were loaded with #1 buckshot. These were also turned over to DS Young.

"An examination of the floor in the laundry room indicated that the glass from the door had been knocked into the room from the outside. A .32-caliber H & R revolver, serial #33959, was observed on the washing machine. The revolver had been on the floor. However, someone had earlier picked it up and placed it on the washing machine. The weapon was not loaded when it was examined. There were several drops of blood on the floor as well as pieces of a jacket zipper that appeared to have come from the suspect's coat. A small ladies' ring was also found on the floor and did not belong to anyone in the residence. Photographs of the entire scene were taken as well as video of the scene and house.

"After completing the above interviews SA Mortenson met Sheriff Walker outside by the suspect's body. The suspect had walked 74 feet from the rear of the house, north to a tree line just north of the house and garage.

"Sheriff Walker had called the Daniels Funeral [Home] of Branford to take the body to the Medical Examiners office in Jacksonville. Dennis Starling, an employee of the funeral home arrived and placed the body in a body bag for transport to the ME's office. The suspect had three syringes in his pocket along with a small pair of wire cutters. There were also three 12-gauge gray-colored shotgun shells in his pockets along with a .32-caliber pistol shell. One of the above syringes had a large piece of aluminum foil wrapped around it and appeared to have something inside the foil. The above contents were sent with the body to the ME's office. DS Young filled out the forms for the request for examination by the ME and faxed them to their office.

"A cursory examination of the suspect's body indicated that he had multiple shell shot wounds to his upper left chest and what appeared to be in the left side of his neck. The suspect's shirt and jacket were soaked with his blood which reportedly came from the neck wound. As the funeral [home] was moving the suspect an examination of the suspect's back was done and did not show any exit or entry wounds of any nature in that area.

"After the funeral service removed the body and the crime scene processing was completed the above deputies and agents left the area.

"It had been reported that the second suspect that had been fleeing arrest had been captured and was now at the Lafayette County Jail."

The van at the graveyard had been stolen, as had the .32-caliber pistol that Franklin carried. The suspect was wanted in several Florida jurisdictions in connection with a series of burglaries and robberies, as well as drug-making activities. When the contents of the aluminum foil were examined, it was found to be crack cocaine.

Inside the van, officers found clothing and other personal items belonging to Franklin. They also found that the van had been set up as a methamphetamine lab.

No charges were filed against Raymond Robert Driver. The shooting was described by a Lafayette County Sheriff's Office spokesman as a classic case of self-defense.

Chapter Eleven
Sunday Morning
Coming Down

"I thank God everyday that I was born in the Southern part of the USA and that our forefathers gave us the right to bear arms to defend ourselves. I pray to God that right is never taken from us." Brenda Hibbitts, September 11, 2000.

Brenda Hibbitts

The blue Dodge van sat on the side of Long Branch Road. To the right, turn-of-the-century headstones stood in rows — huge oaks and sweet gums formed a canopy over the cemetery. Beer cans, liquor bottles, and jars of bootleg hooch littered the floor of the van. The three men and two women in the van were coming down from a week-long drunk.

Five bullet holes pocked the windshield, souvenirs of a long-ago drug deal gone bad. From a distance, the holes formed a pattern like the stars of the Big Dipper. The people in the van were too drunk to realize that the holes made the van stick out like a sore thumb.

The driver, Sandra Lewis, owned the van. Her current boyfriend, Tommie Lee Meadows, sat beside her. Sprawled in the backseat were Cleda Bowling and her new boyfriend, Stephen Pyles. A fifth man was slumped on the floor, moaning and holding his head.

It was Sunday, June 16, 1996, in Laurel County, Kentucky. The nearest town, McWhorter, was twenty miles away.

"That the house?" Meadows asked. Bowling crawled up and looked out the window. High on the mountain, at the end of a long clay road, a house sat by itself. She nodded.

"Soon's they leave," Pyles said, "we gonna make a lick on it."

Meadows, from Tennessee, could never get used to these Kentucky mountaineers. They had the strangest sayings. He knew that Pyles meant they planned to break in and rob the place. If the woman was home, they might do more.

"Let's get outta here," Bowling said. She paused, as if she was gathering her courage, then continued, "I don't think we oughta do it."

Meadows was tired of her whining. After all, she'd set this operation up. Bowling was the only one of the five who had lived here and knew the area.

Even though he hadn't seen the residents leave, Meadows snapped, "Let's ride!" That ought to show the bitch, he thought.

Lewis started the old van and headed up the mountain. Blue smoke trailed from the exhaust as the engine had trouble pulling the van up the grade.

Half-way up they saw a pickup truck leave the house. It came slowly down the grade. When it got close enough, Meadows saw it was a man and a kid. They wore suits and ties, and Meadows guessed they were going to a Sunday School meeting. As he passed, the driver of the truck peered at the ratty van. Meadows thought it might stop and turn around. When it kept going, he breathed a sigh of relief.

After what seemed like an hour, the van made it up the mountain. Lewis parked about 150 yards from the house, using a ledge to shield the van so it couldn't be seen. When she turned it off, a cloud of black smoke choked from the exhaust.

Meadows turned to Bowling and said, "Go check the front door."

She gave him a dirty look, and asked, "Why me?"

He spat a string of obscenities at her and she finally got out. She made her way up the path, walked up the steps, and knocked on the door. When no one answered, Bowling turned and came back to the van.

Meadows and Pyles got out, and all three walked to the house. Once they were on the porch, Meadows kicked the door. It didn't budge, and he yanked at it, then slammed it again with his foot.

Pyles rolled his eyes. "Jesus!" he said. He pulled a hammer out of his pocket and struck the window that was encased in the door. The glass cracked like a gunshot and shattered. Pyles then reached inside, twisted the knob, and opened the door.

As they entered the house, Meadows, a thick man with a barrel chest, took the hammer from Pyles. The smaller man didn't want to make Meadows angry, so he let him keep it. The two men and the woman stood in the doorway for a moment. Then Meadows began moving toward the bedroom down the hall.

In a recent interview, Brenda Hibbitts recalled, "They kicked the door so hard that it broke the drywall around the casing. But it's a solid oak door, and it wouldn't give. So they just broke out the window and came on in. I couldn't believe how fast they got inside."

Hibbitts, wearing a nightgown, was talking on the telephone to her friend, Penny Malone.

A few minutes before, Hibbitts' husband, Glen, and their son, had left for church. She'd worked six days that week, including all day Saturday, so she decided to take Sunday off to relax and catch up on chores around the house. She was putting laundry in the washing machine when she heard the door bang open.

Malone also heard the sound and asked, "What in the world was that?"

"I don't know," Hibbitts answered.

It took another moment before she realized that her house was being invaded.

"Call 911," she whispered to Malone. "They're coming in on me."

Hibbitts was already racing toward the living room. Her purse sat by the sofa, and the homeowner reached into it and pulled out a Smith & Wesson Ladysmith 9mm semiautomatic pistol. "I always keep it in my purse," she said. "You never know when you're going to need it."

Hibbitts, still holding the portable phone, walked straight to the hall and saw three intruders. Even though she was startled, she pointed the gun at them and asked, "What are you doing in my house?"

No one answered.

Later, describing the surreal scene, Hibbitts said, "One guy looked like Tex Cobb, the boxer turned television star. He just stared at me. It was like, this is your house, but what are you going to do about it? I said, 'Get out of my house or I'll shoot you.'"

Standing in the hall with a huge mirror as a backdrop the homeowner faced the intruders. They were about ten feet apart. Still the intruders made no move to leave.

"If you don't get out," Hibbitts repeated, "I'm gonna shoot you."

None of the invaders had spoken a word. Then the big man began to move in her direction. He walked slowly, cautiously, as if feeling his way forward. Then he raised a claw hammer, as if to strike her. It all happened so quickly that the homeowner didn't have time to think. When the assailant was less than five feet away, Hibbitts pulled the trigger.

The explosion rocked the enclosed hall.

"When I shot him, I thought I missed," Hibbitts recalled. "He didn't drop the hammer or change expression. It wasn't like you see on television where they slam backwards and fall. He just stood there. Then all of a sudden all three of the robbers jumped into my bedroom which was across the hall from where they were standing."

One unusual feature about Hibbitts' bedroom was that it had two doors opening into the hall. The invaders had entered the one closest to the oak door they'd broken into.

Once inside the bedroom, the intruders slammed the door shut. Then she heard someone say, "I'm hit. The bitch shot me."

Still standing in the hallway, the homeowner yelled, "Get out of my house! If I have to come in there, I'll kill everyone of you!" She knew they'd have to come out of one of the bedroom doors to leave.

None of the intruders answered, but the homeowner could hear them rummaging about the room. "They ransacked everything in there looking for a gun," Hibbitts said later. "There was a gun case in the bedroom, and they'd opened it hoping to find a weapon."

Hibbitts wasn't sure if there *was* a gun in the room. The day before, she'd asked her 13-year-old son to move his rifle from the closet. It was a .22-caliber with a "thirty-round clip." She was unsure if her son had indeed put the gun in his own bedroom where they usually kept it. "You know how kids are," she said.

Hibbitts recalled, "I positioned myself where I could see both doors and still have some cover in case they came out shooting." She yelled at the intruders a second time, ordering them to come out. If they didn't, she repeated, she was going to come into the room and kill them.

"I could have gone in and killed them all," Hibbitts recalled. "But I was in my nightgown and didn't have any shoes on and the floor was littered with glass. Anyway, I just wanted them to leave."

Finally, the door cracked open. The assailant whom she'd shot stepped into the hall.

"Please don't shoot me again," he begged. "I'll leave if you won't shoot me."

Hibbitts saw that his shirt was soaked with blood.

"It's your choice how you leave," she replied. "But you're going out one way or the other."

Suddenly, the other two intruders bolted out of the second door, and ran outside.

Once again, her assailant began to walk toward her. He looked angry, the hammer still in his hand.

"Uh-uh!" Hibbitts yelled. "You go out the way you came in."

The man turned, and slipped out the front door.

Hibbitts breathed a sigh of relief, and called 911.

Penny Malone had already called.

Laurel County Sheriff's deputy James E. Sparks and Detective Lonnie W. Owens arrived shortly, followed by Kentucky State Police Trooper Marc Hopkins.

"It took just ten minutes for the deputies to arrive," Hibbitts recalled.

Less than an hour after arriving at the scene, investigators received a report that a man with a gunshot wound had arrived at Marymount Medical Center in Marymount, Kentucky. Trooper Hopkins drove to the hospital, leaving Sparks and Owens in charge of the crime scene.

Hopkins interviewed the nurse who had reported the incident. She stated that a blue van had driven into the picnic area adjacent to the hospital and the occupants had dumped the man onto a table. The van, its windshield pocked with bullet holes, then sped off.

As she watched the strange actions of those in the van, the nurse jotted down the license tag number. She then assisted the wounded man to the emergency room. The suspect's name was Tommie Lee Meadows.

As he was undergoing surgery for a bullet wound to the chest, police stopped a blue van with several bullet holes in the windshield. They arrested Sandra Jean Lewis and Stephen D. Pyles. Both were charged with first-degree burglary, first-degree wanton endangerment, and second-degree criminal mischief. According to police, Meadows would be charged with the same crimes when he recovered.

Cleda Bowling was later arrested at her mother's house. Tommy Meadows, the fifth man in the van (no relation to Tommie Lee Meadows), was also arrested.

In an interview with the wounded suspect, investigators learned that the suspects had deliberately chosen Hibbitts' house because she worked at a pawn shop and they thought "there would be guns and gold at her house." During the interview, Tommie Lee Meadows complained that he was "drunk enough to be stupid, but sober enough to remember."

All the suspects later pled guilty to various charges. Tommie Lee Meadows was sentenced to nineteen years. Pyles, Bowling, and Lewis each received ten years. Tommy Meadows got five years.

Hibbitts later recalled, "One of the reasons I didn't shoot more than once was that I thought the small one was a child. He looked to be about 13-years-old. After shooting the one guy, I drew a bead on the second one, but I didn't want to be responsible for killing a child. So I didn't fire. But the child turned out to be the girlfriend of one of the robbers."

Hibbitts, whose house is so far back in the mountains that only locals can find it, has a theory on why her home was chosen for burglary. "I worked at a pawn shop," she recalled, "and the guy I shot had been in there a week before pretending to want to sell a gun. But I noticed he kept looking around, like he was checking out the place. He also kept looking at me, so that I felt uncomfortable. Then he followed me home one afternoon. Well, this [home invasion] happened about a week after that.

"One of my neighbors, who was serving time in the county jail, called me later and told me that they'd been bragging in jail that their plan was to come and kidnap me, and take me to the pawn shop and make me open it. Then they were going to steal all the guns and jewelry they could and kill me as they were leaving."

About gun control, Hibbitts said, "I think anyone would be an idiot to vote for anyone who's in favor of gun control. I tell these people (and lots of them own guns) who'll vote for someone who wants to take away their guns to take your gun with you and just give it up right then. I'm totally opposed to gun control.

"My aunt, who lived in Rhode Island before she died, would call me and talk about how great the security is there. She said, 'The police can be here in five minutes.' I said, 'How long do you think it took these people to get in my house?'"

"The police told me I done more for this community in one morning than they could have done in twenty years. Every house in this area had been robbed, and suddenly robbers here weren't so inclined to go out and break into houses anymore."

"There are people who are against guns because there's [sic] children in the house. But they should teach them what that gun is for, and what it does, and that if you shoot somebody, they don't come back. That's the problem, there's not enough teaching in the home. That's how we taught our son, and it will work for anyone."

"People ask me if I'm sorry I shot that man. I answer, I'm no more sorry than if I had to shoot an injured dog. I didn't ask for them to come into my house and try to hit me with a hammer."

Because Brenda Hibbitts is comfortable with firearms, she was able to survive what might have been a savage murder.

Chapter Twelve
Death of a
Ninja Warrior

"I feel for those who've died because the government took away the guns they needed to protect themselves." Dave Phillips, October 24, 2000.

On Thursday, September 15, 2000, at 1:30 p.m., a young man walked into Crazy Dave's A/1 Pawn & Jewelry in Crystal River, Florida. The man stood five-feet-seven-inches, weighed about 150 pounds, and was of Oriental descent. He looked to be in his mid-20s.

Dave Phillips, sitting behind the counter, watched the customer walk past the jewelry showcase in the center of the store. The young man headed directly toward the guns which were displayed inside a long glass case near the wall.

Phillips, who doesn't like high-pressure sales tactics, gave him plenty of space. But he noticed that the customer was intently focusing on the handguns.

The showroom was large enough to house numerous items — everything from antique furniture to smaller collectibles, such as coins, rare books, and old bottles. Teenagers often came in to browse through the used video games, cassette tapes, and CDs. Guns were just a small part of Phillips' inventory.

This customer seemed different than most. Later, when asked to describe the man, Phillips would say he seemed "spaced-out, edgy, and unstable."

The customer suddenly looked up and said, "I want a Magnum."

In a recent interview, Phillips recalled, "I knew immediately that he didn't know anything about guns because he didn't specify what type of Magnum he wanted."

The shop owner walked to the display case and helped the man decide on a Smith & Wesson .357 Magnum, a model 687 stainless steel revolver with a 4-inch barrel.

"In Citrus County, where I live, there's a three-day waiting period," the shopowner explained, "which meant that since I'm closed Sunday and Monday, he couldn't pick the gun up until the following Tuesday."

When Phillips explained the waiting period, the young man became agitated. He stated that he needed the gun immediately. The shop owner advised him once again of the law and told him that if his application was not approved, his money would be refunded.

The customer finally decided to go ahead with the purchase, using a Visa Gold card to pay for it. He signed his name, Kevin M. C. Fitzsimmons.

When the young man walked out of the store that day, Dave Philips didn't realize that he would become the center of one of the most bizarre cases in the annals of armed self-defense.

A/1 Pawn & Jewelry sits on busy Highway 19, sandwiched between Strickland's Funeral Home and Ray's Bar-B-Que.

The owner, 49-year-old J. David Phillips, had strategically placed several loaded handguns within his reach in case of a robbery. Having a concealed-carry permit, he also kept a hand-sized Beretta model 950 .25-caliber semiautomatic in his pocket. His shooting buddies called it a "nostril gun" because, according to Phillips, "These small-caliber guns are only effective in three places: the nose, the eye, and the ear." Even though it wasn't the optimal gun for self-defense, Phillips always carried it, keeping a round in the chamber just in case.

When the he arrived to open his shop the following Tuesday morning, Phillips found Fitzsimmons waiting at the door. "I opened the store and let him in," Phillips remembered. The Saturday before, the shop owner had filled out the required 4473 form and called it in to the Florida Department of Law Enforcement, which is the FBI contact for gun dealers in the state. In turn, the FBI performed the background check.

Now, with the young man waiting, Phillips called in the NICS check. It came back "conditional refusal." "What that means," Phillips later explained, "is that they don't necessarily refuse him, but it gives them a few more days to do a further background check. The young man was very sullen. He didn't really act surprised, but he seemed spacey, as if he wasn't all there. I explained to him that it didn't mean that he couldn't have the firearm — he just couldn't have it *today*. But he didn't want to accept that."

"How long will it take?" Fitzsimmons demanded.

Phillips explained that the second check usually takes no more than a day. The shop owner suggested that he call back late Wednesday afternoon.

"I want the gun now!"

"Sorry, but you can't have it until the background check is approved," Phillips replied.

Fitzsimmons paused, then checked to make sure no one else was in the store.

"Why don't you sell it to me off the record?" he proposed.

"No way, man!"

Fitzsimmons glowered at the shop owner, then stomped out.

An hour later, Phillips looked out his large storefront window and saw the man driving through his parking lot. This time, however, he didn't stop. Instead, he drove around back, finally parking his van in the parking area adjacent to Strickland's Funeral Home. Then he got out and walked to a patch of woods behind the pawn shop.

Phillips, now highly suspicious of the young man's intentions, walked to a window near the back of the store where he could observe the van. The shop owner jotted down the license number. Then, as a precaution, he telephoned a friend who worked at the Crystal River Police Department. The friend wasn't in, so Phillips left a message asking the officer to run a background check on Fitzsimmons.

By now, the shop owner had decided that he would not sell the handgun to the customer even if he was approved. The young man struck him as unstable and dangerous. Phillips waited a few minutes, then decided to go outside to check on Fitzsimmons. Walking to his Jeep as if to get something from it, he observed the young man. "He was behind my building in some woods," the shop owner recalled. Noticing that Fitzsimmons was staring intently at a huge oak, Phillips said, "This guy just wasn't acting normal. He looked like he was stalking a tree!" Fitzsimmons looked around and saw the shop owner, and they nodded to each other. Then Phillips returned to his shop.

As he sat down on the stool behind the counter, he glanced at the .357 Magnum revolver that he kept on the shelf beside him. He'd positioned it so that he could grab it quickly with his right hand. It was comforting to know that the gun was there in case it was needed. Phillips had heard of too many robberies that turned into murder. He wasn't planning on becoming another statistic.

Phillips waited on several customers, still feeling uneasy about Fitzsimmons. By 1:15 p.m., everyone had left and he was alone in the store.

The shop owner recalled, "Less than two minutes later, the kid comes in and walks rapidly down the aisle toward me. Before I can react, he stops at the counter, pulls this huge blade out of a sheath, and shouts, 'This is a Ninja sword!' The sheath flew away from him and landed on top of the jewelry display counter. Then, in one motion, he stabs me."

As his assailant shoved the sword at him, Phillips pushed backwards, away from the counter. He did so just in the nick of time. The blade of the sword was three feet long. It was officially called a samurai sword. While the edges were thick and dull, the point looked razor-sharp. It dug deep into Phillips' chest, stopping a fraction of an inch from his heart.

As he pitched backwards, Phillips reached out with his right hand for the gun on the shelf beside his stool. But he flew past the shelf and missed the gun.

"[Fitzsimmons] ran around behind the desk," Phillips remembered. "And he stabbed me again in almost the same exact spot. Then he pulled the sword out and stabbed me in the stomach. They were straight-on thrusts. No slashing or cutting, just like the old Army carry thrusts."

The shock of the attack stunned the shopowner, but Phillips managed to pull himself to his feet. Then he watched in horror as the assailant plunged the blade into him again. In a matter of seconds, the shopowner had been stabbed four times.

Phillips, his shirt now drenched with blood, shouted at the assailant, "What are you doing?"

The man didn't answer.

This time, as Fitzsimmons pulled the sword back to stab him again, the shop owner grabbed the blade with his left hand. Using his right hand, he punched his assailant. Fitzsimmons hit back. The struggle, which was centered in the area behind the counter, raged back and forth for several minutes.

"I'm hitting him, he's hitting me," Phillips recalled. "He's punching me with his left fist and hitting me with the hilt of the sword. After it was over I had several bumps on the top of my head and a nasty bruise on my forehead. I was hitting him with my fist, but it had no effect whatever. I'd be very surprised when the toxicology report comes back if he wasn't on drugs."

Phillips knew he was losing his battle for life. If he didn't get medical help soon, he would bleed to death. He remembered, "Everything I'd tried so far hadn't worked. So I decided to distance myself from the threat."

Fitzsimmons yanked the blade of the sword out of Phillips' hand. As the assailant positioned it to stab the shopowner again, Phillips made a dash for his office. With Fitzsimmons breathing down his neck, he bolted inside.

"I slammed the door on him as hard as I could," Phillips remembered. "Again, it had no effect whatsoever. Then he stabbed the sword all the way through the door."

The office had no windows and was dark because the shop owner left the lights off when it wasn't in use. Phillips didn't have time to turn on the lights. Instead, he rushed toward his desk. He knew he had a pistol in the top drawer. In his panic, he still hadn't remembered the little gun in his pocket.

As he ran across the room, he didn't see a jumble of electric wires that littered the floor. He stumbled over them and fell. His head slammed into the desk, knocking his computer to the floor.

The assailant quickly opened the door and bore down on the shopowner again. Phillips barely had time to climb to his feet before Fitzsimmons stabbed him again. This time Fitzsimmons had delivered the telling thrust.

Phillips recalled, "This is where I got my most serious stab wound. He stabbed me right in the gut, through the intestines.

The pain was severe, and he's trying to shove it in further. Somehow, we fight across the floor for another eight or ten feet. I'm holding onto the blade with my left hand while he's trying to shove it in with both hands. I'm trying to pull it out and he's pushing it in."

At that point, Phillips remembered the gun in his pocket.

Describing his feelings when he remembered that he was carrying the gun, Phillips said he became euphoric. He described the feeling as being similar to a religious experience. "There we were," he said, "fighting for the sword, and it's almost like a revelation. I've read stories of the 95-pound woman who pulls the car off somebody, and I always believed it was possible because I believe in God, and anything is possible through God. This was similar, like suddenly there's a light at the end of the tunnel."

Phillips recalled, "I had a death grip on the blade. I was surprised that it didn't slice my hand, though when this was over I had bruises all over both hands." He slowly began to pull the blade out of his body. His "revelation" had given him new strength. Phillips used all the power he could muster, and suddenly wrenched the blade from his stomach.

Now he was free. Still holding the sword with his left hand, Phillips reached into his right pocket and pulled out the pistol. He aimed for his assailant's left eye socket. The shopowner placed the gun only a few inches from Fitzsimmons and pulled the trigger. The little gun popped like a firecracker.

There was no reaction from Fitzsimmons, so Phillips fired again. Suddenly, blood streamed from the face of his attacker. Still holding onto the sword, Phillips fired again. He shot once more. Then he fired his final shot.

"I only remember shooting twice," he said later. "But five shots hit the guy: two in the left eye, and two in the cheek. The final round went through his left hand and plowed through the door in my office."

Phillips continued, "Doctors later said that one bullet went through his brain, and another lodged in his spinal column after bouncing around a little bit. Two went all the way through him and the police found them lying spent on the floor about fifteen feet behind him."

Fitzsimmons suddenly collapsed to the floor. It was only then that the shopowner let go of the sword. Phillips stepped over his assailant and stumbled out of his office. Wading through puddles of blood, he walked back to the counter. Picking up the phone, he dialed 911.

Blood was still pumping from his wounds. The telephone and the counter were smeared with blood. Looking across the floor leading to his office, he saw a trail of crimson. His glasses lay on the floor, in the doorway, the wire frames crunched almost beyond recognition.

His pain was intense. "This wasn't one of those stories where the victim was numb, or immune to the pain," Phillips said. "Every time he stabbed me, it hurt. The last wound to the stomach was excruciating."

While he was still on the line to the dispatcher, three teenagers walked into the store, unaware of the events that had just occurred. Suddenly, police cars were everywhere. The hapless teens were ordered to come out with their hands up. Then they were taken down on the ground, handcuffed, and placed in separate police cars for questioning. Phillips staggered to the door and informed the officers that the teenagers weren't involved.

Ambulances quickly arrived, and the wounded shopowner was placed on a stretcher and driven to the airport a few miles away. He was then transported by helicopter to St. Joseph's Hospital in Tampa.

Phillips endured ten hours of surgery. His intestine, which had been perforated, was sewn back together. His other wounds, though painful, weren't life-threatening. After spending nine days in the hospital, he was released.

Kevin Fitzsimmons died the following day.

Three weeks after being attacked, Phillips returned to his shop.

In a recent interview, he said, "God wasn't done with me yet. I was able to outlast [my assailant], even though I made mistakes. I was really amazed that I stayed on my feet the whole time, except when I was knocked off the stool, and that I never lost consciousness. It was only when I went in for surgery that they put me under."

"I don't know why I didn't think of the gun in my pocket except to say that I carry it every day, just like pocket change, and I simply forgot I had it.

"I was yelling at him. 'Why are you doing this?' I said. 'You're nuts.' My most intense emotion during the whole ordeal was disbelief. Why is this happening? Am I missing something? I was upset. There was no reason for him to come in my store and attack me.

"My wife works at the Citrus County Property Appraiser's Office. After they arrived, one of the officers was sent to get her, and she was able to speak with me before I left for the hospital."

The motive for Fitzsimmons' attack on Phillips entered the realm of the grotesque. "What set him off," Phillips said, "was my refusal to sell him the gun. It screwed up his timetable for committing mass murder. In his van, cops found more than three hundred rounds of .357 Magnum ammunition. They also found a complete Ninja outfit with masks, swords, knives, and throwing stars. And they found a bus schedule to Atlanta with several travel arrangements made for arrival on the 26th."

Investigators later determined that Fitzsimmons was obsessed with Kristina Abernathy, a meteorologist at the Weather Channel, whose offices are in Atlanta. He had written to her, but when she hadn't responded, Fitzsimmons took it as a personal rejection. Based on evidence found in his van, investigators theorized that he planned to go on a shooting spree at the Weather Channel, with his final victim being Abernathy.

Phillips said, "His own mother had gotten a restraining order on him because of his violence. That's the reason for the delay in the approval of the background check. However, if he'd waited just one more day, he would have been approved, because the restraining order was due to expire the very day he attacked me.

"The reason his mother had a restraining order put on him was that he was over at her house when Kristina Abernathy came on and he began stabbing the television with a knife. He ruined the television."

Fitzsimmons, a Korean, had been adopted when he was three years old and had taken the name of his adopted family. He was treated well, and given every opportunity to succeed. However, according to his parents, he never felt like he fit in. It was only in recent months, though, that he'd begun to study karate, and take an interest in Ninja ways. He'd recently started fights at two fast-food restaurants in order to prove his Ninja skills.

Some have called Phillips a hero, but he doesn't think so. "It bothers me that I killed somebody," Phillips said. "I have trouble sleeping at night. I'm going to get counseling because, regardless of how much he deserved it, I can't get over the fact that I took a human life."

Chapter Thirteen
Snapshots

"Don Cook was a very sick, delusional person who actually should have been in prison, but because of our criminal justice system was free to walk the streets..." Elizabeth Magruder, March 4, 2001.

I

Heathrow, located a few miles north of Orlando, Florida, was a gated, security-conscious development consisting of pricey Tudor-style homes, a golf course, lakes, and a clubhouse. Huge old oaks, sweet gums, and Southern pine trees shaded the community. Crime was virtually non-existent.

But on May 10, 1999, at 8:04 a.m., as Ron and Elizabeth Magruder sat outside by the enclosed pool sipping coffee and reading the newspaper, an intruder suddenly entered through a screen door.

Don Cook, a registered sexual predator who was facing trial for raping his own 13-year-old daughter, had been stalking Elizabeth for months.

Now he grabbed the homeowner by the throat and dragged her through the sliding glass door into the house. Ron pursued them into the kitchen, but the assailant pulled out a small-caliber pistol and pointed it at him.

"Who's he?" the gunman demanded.

As his attention turned toward her husband, Cook loosened his grip on Elizabeth. She used the distraction to jerk away from him. Fleeing down the hall toward the master bedroom, she heard Cook sprinting after her. He quickly closed in on her.

"Call 911," Elizabeth yelled to her husband, forgetting that she was holding the portable telephone. Ron Magruder ran to a neighbor's house and called the Sheriff's office.

The stalking had begun in the spring of 1998 when Elizabeth had hired Don Cook, then an employee of Heathrow, to complete a landscaping job. After the work was finished, Cook continued to hang around, even after being ordered to leave. He would call Elizabeth several times a day, and would drive by her house at all hours of the day and night. Eventually, he was fired by Heathrow for harassing Elizabeth.

Still, he continued to stalk her. The former gardener followed her around the golf course, hiding in the bushes and spying on her with binoculars. Once he chased her and a Heathrow employee across the golf course. When she confronted him and told him he was "sick," the former gardener became angry.

Because Cook continued to stalk her, Elizabeth obtained a restraining order from the Seminole County courthouse. A law enforcement officer, understanding the seriousness of Cook's obsession, suggested she arm herself. Magruder, a native of Canada who had never fired a gun, went to a shop and bought a .38-caliber revolver. The officer then took her to a firing range and trained her in how to use the gun.

After the restraining order was issued, Cook's past was unearthed. He was currently awaiting trial for the rape of his own 13-year-old daughter. Because of previous charges of sexual assault on a child, Cook would have been sent to prison for at least ten years had he been convicted. But his lawyer had talked the presiding judge into letting him remain free while he awaited trial.

Now, with the deranged stalker inside her house, Elizabeth Magruder knew it was life or death. She raced to the closet in her bedroom, with Cook only a step behind. She reached up to the shelf where she'd hidden the gun. She got it just in time.

Cook clutched at her, grabbing her by the throat. He pulled her to him, placing her in a choke-hold. As he held her in a death grip, Elizabeth twisted toward him, placed the gun against his chest and squeezed the trigger.

The shot startled Cook. He stepped back, then raised his gun and fired a barrage in her direction. The first shot hit Elizabeth in the arm, breaking it. Her gun clattered to the floor. A second shot hit her in the abdomen.

Elizabeth dodged past Cook and raced back down the hall. A third shot grazed her calf, and a fourth shot barely missed her head. The homeowner finally made it outside, and staggered across the lawn to a neighbor's house for help.

Sheriff's deputies arrived within minutes of being called. After interviewing Elizabeth and Ron, three SWAT team deputies entered the Magruder residence. There they found Donald Cook lying dead on the kitchen floor, a bullet hole in his chest. According to the police reports, "the bullet traveled through the pericardial sac, right lung, diaphragm and liver, lodging in the right chest wall...."

Elizabeth was airlifted to the hospital where she underwent six hours of surgery. She eventually returned home and began taking steps to obtain her concealed-carry permit.

The Canadian now has a great respect for the Second Amendment. "Until we can keep guns out of the hands of criminals," she said. "We absolutely need the right to keep and bear arms to defend ourselves."

II

At exactly 1:51 a.m., on August 9, 2000, a 911 call came in to the Pasco County, Florida, Emergency Communication Center.

Dispatcher: "911."

Caller: "I just shot a man, a man was just in my house, and tried raping me, and I shot him. Oh my God!"

Dispatcher: "Ma'am."

Caller: (The caller screams several times.) "He's still alive. Come quick!"

Dispatcher: "Ma'am, calm down."

Caller: "He's still alive. I heard him in there."

Dispatcher: "All right, what's the address?"

(The caller gave her address.)

Dispatcher: "You say the man broke into your house?"

Caller: "Yes. Oh my God, oh my God, oh my God. I heard him in there."

Dispatcher: "All right. What kind of gun is it?"

Caller: "I don't know. I don't know. Oh my God. Oh my God. How long will it take the police to get here? Oh my..."

Dispatcher: "We're getting an ambulance on the way over right now."

Caller: "Yes, please hurry. He's still alive. He's going to come back after me."

Dispatcher: "All right. Stay on the line. I'm going to put you through to the Sheriff's office. Okay?"

At approximately 1:45 a.m., Maria Pittaras had awakened from a deep sleep. She felt a dead weight on top of her and heard a voice that at first seemed to be coming from a distance. It took her a moment to realize that a man was lying on her.

As her eyes adjusted to the darkness, she screamed.

"Shut up, bitch!"

The intruder grabbed her mouth and squeezed until she quieted. Pittaras felt gloves on his hands.

Now she could make out a silhouette of the man and saw that he wore a mask.

She screamed again and her assailant yelled at her. He placed the blade of a knife against her throat. "Can you feel that, bitch?" he asked.

She nodded.

"Then you better behave," he threatened, spitting out a string of expletives.

The man began ripping the covers off Pittaras.

"Please stop," she begged.

He began to grope her as he removed the covers.

"You know me," he said. "You want me."

Pittaras tried to place the voice. She'd heard it, but couldn't remember where.

"I've seen how you look at me at work," he said.

The homeowner screwed up her courage and responded. "If you know I want you so bad," she said, "then why are you doing this?"

"Shut your mouth, bitch!"

By now the man had removed the covers and was groping her more aggressively. His breath was coming hard.

Pittaras remembered the gun she kept on the nightstand beside her bed. It was a .38-caliber Smith & Wesson five-shot revolver that her father had given her a year before.

After graduating from college, she'd taken a job with Bausch and Lomb as a chemist. A few months earlier, Pittaras had bought her dream house in the upscale Turtle Lakes subdivision. Although she had little time to socialize with neighbors, she felt at home there. She spent her spare time keeping up her house and lawn.

Now, as the intruder struggled with her, she squirmed backward in the bed trying to reach her gun.

Thank God, she thought. There it is!

Using her right hand, she cocked it and fired. In her panic, she missed. The homeowner heard the bullet thud into a far wall.

Damn!

Now Pittaras clamped both hands around the stock. She placed the barrel of the gun against the man's neck and again squeezed the trigger.

He cursed, then slumped down on the bed beside her.

The homeowner then jumped up and fled. She ran to the kitchen, snatched the telephone from the wall and called 911.

When police arrived, they found a man lying on the bed. According to a police report, "The deceased [suspect] was lying on... his back, with his legs over the edge of the bed. I observed the deceased victim to have a large amount of blood around his neck area, and on his shoulder and upper arm... I observed a white net bag, partially over the deceased [suspect's] head, and a glove on [his] left hand, which was lying by his side on the bed. There was a knife lying by his hand..."

Investigators determined that the intruder had used pruning shears to break out a bedroom window and enter the house. He was identified as Robert Metz, a neighbor who lived four doors down from Pittaras.

She recalled that they had spoken once or twice after she first moved into the house. That was her only contact with him.

Metz's wife, Carolyn, stated that he had been taking medication for depression, but had recently stopped. Carolyn had gone to bed that night and awoke to find her husband gone. When she looked outside, she saw the police car lights flashing. It was then that she learned that he'd been shot.

In an interview with the *St. Petersburg Times*, Maria Pittaras said, "I understand that I did what I had to do, but I'm never going to be a normal person again. Every day, I'm going to have to come to terms [with the fact] that I took a man's life, a man with a family."

When talking about the shooting, Pittaras sobbed. "I haven't slept," she said. "I haven't eaten. I feel like I'm frozen." She paused, then continued, "I know I will eventually, someday, put my life back together. I know I'll get past this, but I'll never forget about it. And I don't think I'll ever stop wondering why it had to happen."

III

It was 11:00 p.m., on November 18, 2000.

Seventy-two-year-old Jean Zamarripa later told a crowded courtroom that she "had just said her bedtime prayers" when she heard a strange noise. Living in the Knob Hill section of Colorado Springs, Colorado, she thought it was the rattling of the humidifier.

Zamarripa listened more closely. The rapes of several elderly women in her neighborhood had alerted her to be on the lookout for danger. When she heard a scratching sound on her back porch, then a thump, she knew someone was outside.

The former medical technician picked up the telephone and called 911. Then she hung up, reached beneath her bed, and retrieved a .38-caliber revolver. With her hand trembling, she walked through the house toward the back door. Bracing the gun on the kitchen counter, Zamarripa aimed it where she thought the intruder would enter.

As she waited, the widow thought of the other rapes she'd read about. Just a few months before, a fifty-six-year-old woman had been coming out of her bathroom at about 11:00 p.m. when a masked intruder grabbed her. He tied her hands and feet, then took off her clothes and repeatedly raped her. After the rapes, he forced her to take a bath. Then he told her that all women fantasize about being raped. Like he's doing her a favor, thought an indignant Zamarripa.

In nearby Security, a fifty-one-year-old woman was also accosted by a masked man as she left her bathroom. She fought him, but ended up being choked and stabbed in the neck and abdomen. The rapist then assaulted her for hours. After the rapes, he swabbed beneath her legs with a damp towel and a household disinfectant.

The same rapist was also suspected of having assaulted a 76-year-old woman who lived a few doors down from Zamarripa.

As she stood holding the gun, the homeowner braced herself for the confrontation. Outside, she heard the man pull down the storm door. A moment later, her back door crashed open. The invader had broken two locks, including a deadbolt. He'd obviously slammed against it with his shoulder since his momentum knocked him to the floor.

Zamarripa never adjusted her aim. The intruder began to rise.

BOOM! BOOM! BOOM!

Gunshots roared inside the little room.

In later testimony, Zamarripa said, "In 72 years, I had never lived through anything like it. The only way I can describe it is sheer terror... [But] I knew if I didn't shoot him, he would have raped me."
The man turned to run, and the homeowner fired once more. As suddenly as he appeared, the invader was gone. Zamarripa heard a car start up, then she again picked up the telephone.

Anthony Allen Peralez was quickly arrested by police after sideswiping several vehicles while fleeing Zamarripa's residence.
In addition to three bullet wounds, officers found a "rape kit" in his car. At his trial, prosecutors produced gloves, a ski mask with holes for the eyes and mouth, and a small black flashlight. DNA taken from each victim matched DNA taken from one of Zamarripa's bullets that passed through Peralez's shoulder. The bullet, coated with Peralez's blood, was a key piece of evidence in the trial that followed.
Prosecutor John Newsome summed up the savagery of the assaults. "All the attacks involved tremendous violence," he said. "He slit [one victim's] throat. He beat [another] within an inch of her life..."
Speaking of Zamarripa, Newsome said, "It was only because he was shot and ran from her house, bleeding, that she wasn't a rape victim."
Peralez, who had four previous convictions for violent crimes, was convicted on fifty-one charges. It was later determined by the court that he was a habitual criminal, having previously been convicted of violent crimes on four separate occasions. The serial rapist was sentenced to four life sentences.

After the trial, Zamarripa stated that she was grateful she had a gun. "The only thing I can say to anyone," she said, "is you can never let your guard down... at any age."

As if still puzzled by the sequence of events, Zamarripa paused, then said, "I'm just a little grandmother, and I mind my own business. What would I have done if I hadn't had my gun? I would have been just another statistic."

IV

On the morning of November 17, 1994, Barbara Ravalee cracked her screen door to take a piece of paper from a man who claimed to have a note from her teenage daughter. Alicia was supposed to be in school, not writing notes to a stranger's son, as the man claimed. But as she read the crinkled sheet the man had given her, she knew something was wrong. It wasn't Alicia's handwriting.

Before Ravalee could turn to confront the man, he pushed through the door.

Ravalee, recuperating from surgery in her Harvey, Illinois, home, was barely able to stand. Only the man's insistent ringing of the doorbell had caused her to get out of bed. Her two-year-old son, Kendall, had followed her upstairs from her basement bedroom. Now he was pulling at her leg. Her eleven-year-old son, Eric, slept in another bedroom.

The stranger, later identified as Johnny Jones, raised a rusty knife in the air, and suddenly stabbed Ravalee. As she raised her hand to protect herself, the man sliced her palm. Now she brought both arms up over her head in an attempt to deflect the next blow. But the intruder lowered the knife and stabbed her in the side. Then he pulled it out and stabbed her again.

Things were happening in slow motion. Ravalee could even see the blood on the blade as the assailant pulled it out of her body and plunged it into her again and again.

She screamed.

In recent weeks, she'd been so concerned about the safety of her family that she'd bought a gun, a five-shot .38-caliber revolver. Three recent burglaries of her home frightened her. In fact, it seemed that someone was watching her house and striking only when no one was home. Unfortunately, the pistol was under her mattress and had been secured with a trigger lock.

By now, the fight had moved back into the kitchen. Between her screams and Kendall's wild shrieks, the attacker uttered a quiet sentence. "I'm gonna kill you," he said. He stabbed her again, and she fell.

She lay on her back, trying to kick the knife out of the man's hands. Each time she kicked, though, he sidestepped her blows and jabbed the knife into her legs.

Ravalee looked and saw Eric coming down the stairs. The 11-year-old only hesitated for a moment, then threw his scrawny body on the back of the man who was stabbing his mother.

As her son tried to choke the man, he was distracted enough for Ravalee to rise to her feet. The man bit Eric, almost taking off his thumb. As the boy wailed, Ravalee rushed forward to help.

The intruder saw her coming and swung the knife at her. Like a haymaker punch, the blade landed squarely in her right eye. She went weak, and blood began spurting from the eye. The pain was almost unbearable.

Eric was still on the man's back, holding him for dear life.

Ravalee knew now that the only chance for her family to survive was for her to get the gun. She suddenly sprinted away from the battle, heading back down the stairs. As she reached the bedroom, the howls and shrieks of her sons tortured her.

She opened the door and raced into the room. Ravalee grabbed the gun. Then she saw the trigger lock.

Damn!

Her right eye was blind. Her hands weren't working well. She was drenched in blood. And now she was fumbling with a stupid trigger lock. She bit at it, yanked at it, clawed at it, but nothing helped. Oh God, a man was killing her kids and there was nothing she could do about it.

Then she remembered the key. She'd hidden it underneath her exercise machine. She raced for the machine, grabbed the key, and finally freed the gun from its trigger lock.

She bolted back up the stairs.

The battle that had begun near the front door and spilled into the kitchen was now raging in the living room. Eric lay on a table while the intruder beat him with an iron plant holder.

"Get away from my children!" she screamed.

He looked at her. Seeing the pistol in her hands, his eyes widened. Ravalee didn't want to shoot her son, so she fired a shot into the ceiling.

The man jumped up, turned and ran back toward the kitchen. She lost sight of him, but heard him stumbling around her kitchen.

Ravalee followed. She briefly saw him run into the dining room. When Ravalee caught sight of him again, he'd raised his hands to knock out a window.

She assumed the combat stance and fired. And fired. And fired. And fired.

As the intruder crumpled to the floor, she continued to pull the trigger. Clickclickclickclickclick. Why won't it shoot anymore? she wondered.

Her assailant lay on the floor. He looked up at her, and croaked, "Please don't shoot me again." She noticed his voice sounded as high as a woman's. She also noticed blood spurting out of his chest.

Finally, Ravalee realized the reason the gun wouldn't shoot anymore was because she'd run out of ammunition.

She yelled for Eric to call 911. Then she stood guard over the intruder.

Police arrested Johnny Jones and placed him in a hospital. He was paralyzed from the chest down, effectively ending a lifetime of crime. The 37-year-old Jones had spent eighteen of his last 20 years in prison. He'd been convicted of rape on two occasions, and later confessed to two murders.

At the trial, Ravalee testified against Jones, recounting the desperation of her fight. She sobbed as she told of the bravery of her children in fighting off the unprovoked attack. A jury took slightly more than 45 minutes to convict Jones.

In sentencing him to life without parole, Judge Paul J. Nealis issued a statement. "The defendant is a menace," he said, "a career criminal, an urban predator."

Ravalee and Eric eventually recovered from their wounds.

After the shooting, police confiscated her .38-caliber, so Barbara Ravalee went out and bought another one. The first thing she did when she got it was to throw away the trigger lock.

Chapter Fourteen
A Very Rare
Incident

"I hated guns, all of them." Susan Gonzalez, July 17, 2000.

At 12:40 a.m., on August 2, 1997, Susan Gonzalez sat on the sofa in the living room of her rural Jacksonville, Florida, home. The television set was murmuring — she kept it low because her husband, Mike, slept in the bedroom.

She was waiting up for her teenage son. He was at a friend's house, playing video games, and Susan had called him at midnight, ordering him to come home. But he'd talked her into letting him stay for one more hour.

Now, as she waited, she heard the doorknob jiggle and figured it was her son. In a recent interview, Susan said, "I got up off the couch, which is about six feet from the door, to let him in. Halfway to the door, I paused because I hadn't heard his alarm go off. [The burglar alarm on his truck would beep when he locked it.] It kind of stopped me in my tracks as to why he hadn't set his alarm. Then all of a sudden, I heard this really loud, loud noise. It was the door being kicked in."

The door burst open and she stood face-to-face with two masked men. It was so unexpected and frightening that she was frozen. But only for an instant.

She recalled, "I turned to run, screaming, 'Help, Mike, help!' Mike had gone to bed a couple of hours earlier since he had an early shift the following morning. He was in a pretty sound sleep. I made it to the bedroom and slammed the bedroom door but before I could actually get it to shut, they were on the other side beating on it."

The invaders wore camouflage clothing, gloves and homemade masks. "One mask," Susan explained, "was made of cut-off pants with holes cut for the eyes. The other man had made his from a knit shirt."

Susan, still screaming, pushed against the door as hard as she could. But the two men put their shoulders against it and it suddenly crashed down on Susan. She lurched back, away from the intruders. Through the dim light, they looked like Halloween monsters.

"We later discovered they had two nine-millimeters and a short shotgun of some kind," Susan said. "They also had extra magazines for their handguns because after it was over the police found a clip inside my house. At the time, though, I just seen guns pointing at me. We later learned that they made their living doing violent home invasions. One guy was named Robert Walls, and the other was Raymond Waters. I never saw the getaway driver, Louis Wright."

The invaders began firing. Quick staccato explosions shattered the silence of the room. Susan was hit in the chest and knocked backwards.

"I've heard people say it doesn't hurt," Susan said. "But that bullet felt like fire going through my body."

By this time, Mike had awakened. He jumped out of bed and was headed toward the attackers when he was hit.

Susan said, "He grabbed a hold of both intruders and began fighting them. My husband's a small guy, maybe five-foot-six, but he's stocky and very muscular. Later, he had knots all over his head where they'd beat him with guns."

Mike, bleeding from a gunshot wound to the shoulder and from the beating, managed to push the men out of the bedroom. They struggled into the kitchen, fighting wildly.

Mike seemed to be trying to push the intruders out of the house. They wrestled past the refrigerator and into the living room.

"As soon as they left the room," Susan said, "I grabbed the phone and called 911. All I gave the dispatchers at that point was our address. I told them we were being shot and to get here quick. Then I hung the phone up."

Susan had resigned herself to the fact that she and her husband were going to die. With her call, she hoped to give the police enough time to get there so they could arrest the assailants.

As soon as she hung up, the phone rang. "It was 911 calling back," Susan explained. "During the whole struggle the phone was ringing and the television was going."

Her husband's gun, a 9mm Ruger, was lying on the headboard above the bed.

"I was always against guns," she recalled. "I didn't want them in the home and had requested that they all be locked in the gun cabinet. But about a week and a half earlier, Mike had taken it out and set it on the headboard. He told me how to use it. 'Take the safety off,' he said, 'then cock it.' He emphasized that. I had shot a couple of times, but I would shut my eyes and pull the trigger. I guess he repeated a thousand times, 'Take the safety off and cock it.' We'd argued about it. I wanted to know why we needed a gun in the house. He'd say to defend yourself in case someone breaks in."

Now Susan picked up the gun. She did exactly as Mike had instructed her. She clicked the safety off, then cocked the gun.

"They were still fighting at this point," Susan said. "I didn't know where they were because I was still in the bedroom, but I could hear them. I was afraid that if I came out and shot, I might kill my own husband. I knew I couldn't live with that, but I knew I had to do something to help him."

Susan crept into the kitchen. Seeing the desperate struggle that was taking place by the couch she had vacated only moments before, she thought: If I shoot up above their heads, they're going to know I've got a gun and then they'll leave. "But I guess criminals don't think like the rest of us," she said.

She raised the gun and fired three shots into the ceiling. The bullets pierced the plaster, forming little clouds of dust.

Recalling the horror of the moment, Susan said, "As soon as I fired, one of the men [later determined to be Waters] jerked away from my husband and began running towards me. I ran back into the bedroom thinking he would be right behind he. But he wasn't there."

Susan peeked out the bedroom door. She recalled, "I saw the intruder squatting by the refrigerator. He was waiting for me to come out. I couldn't see his face or mask, but I saw his elbow and arm and gun. I was thinking, if I go out into the kitchen, he's gonna shoot me. But I knew something the intruders didn't know. The kitchen wall has a door about six inches from my bedroom and that door leads back to my dining room. From where he was hiding behind the refrigerator, he couldn't see me when I entered the dining room through that door. Then the dining room leads to the living room."

Susan edged into the kitchen. Then she slipped through the door and entered the dark dining room. A curtain separated it from the living room. She parted the drapes and peered out. Walls, still fighting with her husband, didn't notice her.

But Susan saw the intruder squatting by the refrigerator, his back towards her. He was holding his gun with both hands. It was aimed at the spot she would have had to come to if she'd come into the kitchen. Her plan had worked.

He never saw her. She was about six feet away when she opened fire. She fired seven shots, though at the time she didn't realize it. "I just pulled the trigger until the gun was empty," Susan recalled. "Then I threw the gun down on the floor and turned and seen this guy put his gun to my husband. Boom! Mike dropped. He'd been shot through the side. Then the guy turned toward me and started firing. That's when he got me in the shoulder. I had turned to run and the bullet went through the back of my shoulder and came out the front."

Susan raced back into her bedroom. "It was my safe haven at this point," she said.

She didn't see it, but Waters, with the help of Walls, had stumbled out the door and collapsed in her driveway. She recalled, "The doctor who did the autopsy later told me he would have lived maybe five to ten minutes. I understand one bullet went through the back of his neck and the other in the back near the shoulder blade. The autopsy showed that that bullet went into a lung and the esophagus. According to the autopsy, both bullets would have been fatal."

Susan hid in the closet. She recalled, "At that point, I knew that I was dying." Her whole body was drenched in blood, and the pain in her chest and shoulder made her feel faint.

"I had done everything I knew I could do," she continued. "So I [began] making my peace with the Lord. Out loud. I was asking for forgiveness of my sins, and asking that my husband be okay. I was just talking out loud to Jesus. That was my passage to heaven and I knew that. I knew the Lord wasn't going to turn me away because I had shot this man who had just shot me. But I still had to make my peace with Him and ask for forgiveness of my sins."

After her prayers, everything grew silent.

Suddenly, the phone rang again. Susan, who had taken refuge in her closet, was afraid to answer it. Her answering machine clicked on and the party on the other end of the line hung up. "We later found out it was the dispatchers trying to call," she said. "We also determined that it took the police about fourteen minutes to get here."

Investigators later determined that when Walls saw that their ride had fled, he panicked.

Waters was in no condition to panic. He was dying. He lay on his stomach in the driveway, panting for each breath. His moans further spooked Walls.

"Shut up!" he screamed.

But it did no good. The dying man ignored him.

Susan recalled, "Without realizing it, [Walls] raised his mask up. Then he come back in the house. The first time I knew my husband was alive was when I heard the guy scream, 'Where is the key to that truck?' He used every profanity you could think of. My husband said, 'In the bedroom in my hat on the gun cabinet.' I thought, Oh no, he's coming back in here."

Susan continued to recount the events of that night. "The door was still busted in the bedroom," she said. "And there was still no light in there except the nightlight in the bathroom. I heard [Walls] come in the door. And I heard him stop. I don't know if he stopped because he didn't realize that I was out of ammunition — he didn't know what he was coming back to. But he screamed, 'Where are you?' What he didn't know was that I was about three feet from him. I thought, if you don't say nothing, he'll leave. Well, it didn't work that way."

Walls was desperate. Now he inched into the bedroom.

The confrontation is etched in Susan's mind. "Then he saw me," she recalled. "He took a shotgun with a pistol grip and put it directly against the temple of my head. He said, 'Gimme the keys to that truck.' So I went to my purse to get the key. I got it from there instead of out of Mike's hat because I knew it was the only key on the ring. I guess it was a woman thing. He wouldn't have the keys to my house and other cars if I gave him that one. He kept screaming and cursing at me and I kept begging him not to kill me. I told him I'd already been shot, please don't shoot me anymore. I told him, 'Just take the keys and go." He says, 'Did you call 911?' And I said, 'No. Just take the keys and go.'"

The invader snatched the key from Susan, and turned to leave. At that point, in the light from the kitchen, she saw his face. It was a perfect silhouette, one she'll never forget. "If he'd realized I could identify him," she said, "I think he'd have blown me away." Then he was gone.

"I gave it a few seconds," Susan remembered. "I waited just long enough to know he was gone, then I ran to the living room and looked out the front window. I seen the tail lights going out of the driveway. Then I ran toward the ringing phone and grabbed it. It was the dispatchers. I was screaming, 'Help me. Help me!'"

The dispatchers attempted to calm the hysterical woman, but she kept yelling, "We're shot! We've been shot!"

Then she realized her son would be coming home at any moment. Susan calmed down enough to tell the operators to have the police stop her son before he got there. "I knew he couldn't come in and see what had happened," she later said.

Susan moved toward her husband, afraid of what she would find. Mike was lying beside the sofa.

He whispered, "Help me, I've been shot."

Susan told him, "I've been shot, too. But I've called 911 and they're coming."

She later recalled, "He asked me to go get him a towel. So I get up off the couch and there's glass everywhere. I'm walking barefoot through it. I went back and got a towel. I was so afraid to look at him that I just dropped the towel on him. I wouldn't look. It was about that time I seen blue lights flashing on my wall."

"I ran to the front door," she continued. "I didn't know at the time that the guy was laying in the yard. The first cop there yells, 'Is it just you and your husband here?' I said, 'Yeah, but I shot one of them.' The cop walks up and almost steps on the guy. He jumped. It nearly scared him to death. Then he aimed his gun at the guy. He told me he couldn't help me right now, but that help was on the way. He was kind of my lifeline at that point. Then the next thing I know people are everywhere." Soon the house was filled with police officers and medical personnel.

Mike was taken by ambulance to the hospital. Doctors later informed Susan that the first bullet had hit him in the right shoulder and had exited near his spine. The second bullet, fired point-blank into his side, had also come out near the spine. Miraculously, neither had hit any vital organ and both had missed the spinal column.

Susan wasn't so lucky. She was airlifted to the hospital. Although the two bullets that struck her also exited, her injuries were more extensive. Her lung had collapsed and several ribs were broken. Doctors believe that the lung was punctured by a broken rib as the door caved in on her. Her heart was also bruised, causing massive swelling and shortness of breath.

"The first time I spent seven days in the hospital," she recalled. "Then they let me come home for three days. Then I went back in for lung surgery due to complications. I remember the doctor explaining it to me like this: Your lung is like an orange and we actually had to go in and peel the dried blood from around the lung. There were other complications as well. I now have an 18-inch scar, looks like a shark bite, across my stomach." Several bullet fragments remain inside her body.

The night she arrived at the hospital, Susan kept asking the doctors and the victim's advocate to let her talk to the "boy" she shot. She recalled, "I wanted to ask him, why did you do this to me? I guess my mind works different than a criminal's, so I wanted to know why? I wanted to ask, what have I done to you? I don't even know you. For hours, nobody would tell me I'd killed him."

Susan was finally told that the man she'd shot had died. In addition to having been shot twice, Waters had been run over by Walls as he fled in Mike's pickup truck.

Susan and Mike eventually recovered from their wounds.

When they came home, they found 42 bullet holes in their home. Glass was broken, walls were caved in, and doors were smashed. "It was a wreck," she said.

She later recalled, "We do know from evidence that came out in court that they'd done these home invasions in the past. They were very good at what they did. And they were extremely violent. They almost killed several people. They just didn't know they were going to run into two people who would fight back. I've always been a very fearful person. I think it came from the fact that when I was ten years old a man attempted to kidnap me. He told me to get in his car and even held up a bloody sheet. I ran away. So I didn't know I had it in me to fight back."

Robert Walls was convicted of numerous charges and sentenced to five concurrent life terms. Susan said, "He was charged with one felony murder for the boy I killed; he got another life sentence for attempted first-degree murder for the attempt on my life; he got a life sentence for the attempted murder of my husband; he received a life sentence for armed robbery; and a life sentence for armed burglary." Because of previous convictions, he has no possibility of parole.

Louie Wright, the getaway driver, pled not guilty to armed robbery and turned state's evidence. He got five years and is due to get out of prison early in 2002.

Susan Gonzalez now has a concealed-carry permit and takes a gun with her wherever she goes. Her feelings about firearms changed dramatically on that night.

"I always hated guns," she said. "I was fearful of guns. You hear the tragic stories of people being shot and killed, of children being killed, and I never heard the other side of the story. With five children in the house, I didn't know if I had a child who might kill himself."

"I now have learned to respect guns. I have grandchildren coming to my home and I know they can't get to my gun because I'm a responsible adult. You should train children to respect guns."

"I went and did several television shows in Washington, D.C., and New York City and you can't take a gun up there. I almost didn't do those shows."

She paused and continued, "I believe in our Second Amendment rights now, and I believe that nobody should take that right from me. I don't even believe I should have to get a permit. I think I have a God-given right to carry a gun for self-protection. However, after doing all these television shows and telling everybody I carry a gun, I felt like it would be better if I got a permit. So I did."

Some people feel differently. In July 2000, the *Florida Times-Union* interviewed a spokesperson for the Center to Prevent Handgun Violence. Nancy Hwa stated that "incidences [sic] like Ms. Gonzalez's are very rare. People have to weigh the risks of losing a TV, jewelry or whatever versus losing their life."

According to Gonzalez, Hwa ignores thirteen studies done in the last twenty years which indicate that anywhere from several hundred thousand to two million people successfully defend themselves with firearms each year.

Regardless of the statistics, Susan Gonzalez believes that she and Mike would be dead had they not had a gun. "I feel like I have a right to self-defense," she said, "and I feel that other people do, too."

One question remains. Why didn't Walls shoot Susan when he had the drop on her? The shotgun he held to her head was fully loaded, according to police.

Unless he talks, no one will ever know. But we can guess. In his panic to flee the scene, he didn't want to waste a second. He had forgotten that he'd pulled his mask up so that Susan had a perfect view of his features. Like she said, had he realized she could identify him, he would have had no hesitation in shooting her.

But he was in such a hurry to leave that he let her live.

Susan and Mike now have burglar bars on their home. They keep guns at hand at all times.

"Reality set in when I was shot," Susan said.

Afterword

Each story described in this book is documented by police reports, court documents, newspaper accounts, and — in many cases — interviews with the victims. This collection describes just a few of the thousands of cases of armed self-defense that I've collected in the last few years.

Before the advent of the Internet, it was easy for those who favor additional legal restrictions or an outright ban on firearms to spread the lie that self-defense with guns is "rare." After all, the national media refuse to report such stories.

Cases of self-defense are carried almost exclusively by local newspapers. It is impossible for one person or even a group of individuals to search manually for such stories through each of the 16,000 daily and 6,000 weekly newspapers that exist in America. So, before the Internet became widely available to most people, these cases went largely unnoticed. (This lack of national publicity, of course, contributes to a distorted view of the gun issue.)

I went online four years ago as I was working on my first book, *The Best Defense: True Stories of Intended Victims Who Defended Themselves With a Firearm* (Cumberland House Publishing Company, 1998). The Internet opened up a whole new way to research these stories.

Many newspapers have free online services. Using key words to access their archives and search engines, or scanning the "local" section every day, the researcher can locate stories which have been reported locally. I began gathering cases in this way, first hundreds, then thousands.

Another benefit of the Internet is the ability to meet other like-minded individuals. Soon after my book came out, KeepAndBearArms.com came online. This organization serves the pro-gun community in several capacities. Its director, Angel Shamaya, and I began discussing ways of publicizing and archiving self-defense stories that the mainstream media continued to ignore. It was through this collaborative effort that Operation Self-Defense was formed.

Volunteer members of Operation Self-Defense (called net detectives) spend a few minutes each day scanning local newspapers for stories of armed self-defense. The stories are usually displayed for a day or two on the main page of KeepAndBearArms.com's web site, then archived for future reference. Any researcher is free to use this service simply by logging on. As each story is found, it is forwarded to interested parties in the mainstream media and academia. Because of this, many of these stories have begun to pop up in national publications. A few have even appeared on national television news programs, something unheard of a few years ago. As more and more of these stories are found, it will eventually become impossible for the mainstream press to ignore them.

The importance of national publicity for stories of armed self-defense cannot be overemphasized. While the drumbeat for further encroachments on the ownership of guns has grown louder among some politicians and gun control groups, polls show that large majorities of Americans agree that we have a Constitutional right to own guns. Even larger majoritics feel that self-defense is both a Constitutional as well as an inalienable right.

For this reason, those who favor additional restrictions on guns refuse to discuss self-defense issues. They would like to see these cases remain buried in local newspapers. Before the formation of Operation Self-Defense, this was indeed the case.

With only a few volunteers scanning about two hundred newspapers each day, Operation Self-Defense has begun to change the debate on guns.

As an example of the work done by net detectives, here are a few representative cases found by searches in a five-day period from December 3 to December 8, 2001. (How many additional cases would be found if we could search every daily newspaper each day as well as all weekly newspapers?)

1. On December 3, 2001, Tommy Banks and David Price robbed a Jackson, Mississippi, gas station, shooting a customer who entered the store unexpectedly. Then, as they fled on foot, the two forced their way into the home of Charles Suddeth. The armed men robbed the homeowner of his car keys, but they got stuck as they tried to drive away. For some reason, they then ran back to the house. Suddeth, who had retrieved his handgun, opened fire, driving the robbers into the hands of police who were rushing toward the scene. The two thugs were arrested and charged with numerous crimes, including the first-degree murder of the customer.

2. On December 4, Craig R. Swenson of La Center, Washington, was shot to death. After sustaining a vicious assault from her husband, Cheryl Swenson ran into the master bedroom, locked the door, and dialed 911. Before police could arrive, however, Swenson broke down the door. By now, Cheryl had retrieved a Magnum .357-caliber handgun. As Swenson advanced in a threatening manner, the abused wife blasted him dead. Cheryl Swenson was not charged with any crime.

3. On December 4, a Baker, Louisiana, robber was killed and a homeowner wounded in a shootout between residents and home invaders. Two unidentified masked intruders burst through the door and forced two female residents to lie on the floor. After tying the women up, they forced the two male occupants to the back of the house. One resident grabbed a handgun and began firing. In an exchange of gunfire, one robber was killed and one resident slightly wounded.

4. On December 5, J.H. Lynn, an off-duty Houston, Texas, police officer, confronted two men who were stealing concrete statues from his yard. They jumped in their car, as if to flee, then one of the thieves turned and pointed a handgun at Lynn. The officer fired one shot, causing them to flee. They were later arrested and charged with various crimes. Lynn's actions were ruled justified.

5. On December 5, an elderly Camden, Arkansas, man awoke to find an intruder in his home. After the unidentified resident was attacked by the assailant, he was able to get his gun. He opened fire, wounding the invader. The homeowner was not charged.

6. On December 5, Lakeland, Florida, shopkeeper John Samanns shot a burglar who threatened him with a crowbar. Samanns was in his office when he heard a burglar alarm sound. The businessman retrieved a Taurus 9mm semiautomatic handgun and went to investigate. He found Larry D. Russell inside the store and, when the burglar approached him with a crowbar raised in the air, the shopowner fired. Russell died at the scene. Police said Samanns acted within his rights and would not be charged.

7. A store video recorded a self-defense shooting in Van Buren Township, Michigan. According to a December 6 story in the *Ann Arbor News*, two men wearing plaid jackets, hoods, and masks entered the store carrying a rifle. As they attempted

to rob the owner, he pulled out a handgun and opened fire, causing the would-be robbers to flee. The storeowner, who had a permit to carry a concealed weapon, was not charged.

8. On December 6, a would-be robber was thwarted when Erin Moul, owner of Cover to Cover Books, pulled a handgun. The robber entered the store, looked around for a few minutes, then approached the cash register. He demanded that Moul open the register and give him the money. "I don't think so," she said, and whipped a 9mm semiautomatic pistol out of her purse. The robber fled. Moul, who has a permit to carry a concealed weapon, said the robber "freaked out" when he saw her gun.

9. On December 6, eighty-three-year-old Minnie Dorsey fought off a burglar in her Sanford, Florida, home. The intruder, whom she labeled a "rock star" — i.e., a crackhead — demanded that she give him money. But the feisty grandmother refused and pulled her .32-caliber handgun. After a brief struggle in which Dorsey was shot in the thumb and grazed in the forehead, the intruder fled. Dorsey, who lives in a ghetto and has a fenced yard, a padlock on her gate and another on her door, as well as other security features around her home, stated that the intruder kicked in the door and threatened her. Summing up the incident, she said, "He didn't get my money. He thought I was going to run, but he's the one who ran." Dorsey was not seriously injured in the attack.

10. On December 6, in Charlotte, North Carolina, Amber Moultrie pulled a knife on Caressa Bess. A long-standing feud between the women came to a head when Moultrie slashed Bess. The victim pulled out a handgun and shot Moultrie. Bess, who acted in self-defense, was not charged.

11. On December 8, in Birmingham, Alabama, a robber was shot by a homeowner during a robbery attempt.

12. On December 8, the *Kentucky Post* featured a story about a "serial robber" who was shot and killed a few days earlier by a shopkeeper. Perry Pinkelton had attempted to rob the Twelfth Street Deli Mart in Covington. Pinkelton exchanged gunfire with a clerk and was fatally wounded. The clerk was not injured and no charges were filed against him. Police stated that Pinkelton had committed numerous crimes.

These twelve stories run the gamut: the domestic shooting of an abusive husband; robbers thwarted by store clerks and business owners; residents who faced down home invaders and won; and a citizen who survived a knife attack because she had a handgun.

Four of the intended victims were women. At least one was black. At least one was Oriental, and another was Indian.

Self-defense is an equal opportunity emancipator.

Fate reversal. How many lives were saved by the heroic actions of those I've written about in this book? How many innocent victims were never assaulted? How many women were never raped? Can we place a value on property never stolen?

It's impossible to say, but I made an educated guess.

Beginning with the cases presented in the Preface and ending with those in the Afterword, I counted forty-six stories in which victims stopped criminal acts. My estimate of *future* criminal acts stopped by these armed citizens are:

Murders prevented — 85
Rapes prevented — 38
Assaults prevented — 54
Property losses prevented — $925,000

Using the first case in my book as an example, I'll explain how I arrived at my figures. (I invite readers to do their own count and send me their results.) Had Adrian Rodricka Cathey not been stopped, there is no doubt that he would have continued raping young college women. Experts have determined that serial rapists assault an average of twenty women before being caught. Subtract four women that he actually raped from twenty and you have sixteen. I think it is not unlikely that he would have raped at least that many women — many rapists have assaulted upwards of one hundred before being arrested.

Cathey had also been charged (though not convicted) with three counts of attempted murder. His violent propensities would no doubt have finally led to him to kill. So I estimate he would have murdered at least three women. (I did not count his physical assaults — i.e., with a knife — in the final tally because they would have overlapped the rape counts.) I also didn't add property crimes to his count because there is no indication that he stole items from the homes he entered.

Think about it.

Had not an armed citizen intervened in these forty-six cases, eighty-five people who are alive today would have been murdered. Thirty-eight women would have been subjected to the degradation and brutality of rape. Fifty-four innocent citizens would have been violently assaulted. And nearly one million dollars in property would have been stolen.

I invite the reader to make his or her own estimate of criminal acts that were never committed in these cases. Write me and let me know what you come up with. My figures are estimates at best, but I'll send you a detailed chart showing how I arrived at them.

You can write to me at the following address: Robert A. Waters, PO Box 771509, Ocala, Florida 34477-1509. Or visit my Web page at http://www.robertwaters.net.

Robert A. Waters

Robert A. Waters received his Bachelor of Science degree from Middle Tennessee State University and his Master of Education Degree from the University of Georgia. He worked for 25 years with the developmentally disabled before taking early retirement in order to write full time. His first book, *The Best Defense: True Stories of Intended Victims Who Defended Themselves With a Firearm,* was published in 1998. Since then, he has published numerous articles in publications as diverse as the *Detroit News, Ocala Star-Banner, American Guardian,* and the *Sierra Times.* Waters has two grown children. He lives in Ocala, Florida, with his wife of thirty years.

YOU WILL ALSO WANT TO READ:

☐ **19188 PERSONAL DEFENSE WEAPONS, by J. Randall.** The author, a private detective and weapons buff, evaluates all kinds of weapons: guns, knives, sticks, gas canisters, martial arts weapons, and many others — by asking some very interesting questions: Is it too deadly to use? Is it illegal to carry? Can it be comfortably concealed? How much skill does it take? Is it reliable? Whatever your situation, this practical book will help you find protection you can live with. *1992, 5½ x 8½, 102 pp, illustrated, soft cover.* **$12.00.**

☐ **19197 STREET SMARTS FOR THE NEW MILLENNIUM, by Jack Luger.** Life can be risky for the average citizen. There are criminal elements in our society, which pose real dangers to the safety and security of ourselves and our families. In this unique book, author Jack Luger has provided the methods and resources that enable the reader to minimize these threats to our lives, liberties, and pursuit of happiness. You'll learn to: depend on personal resources instead of police; protect yourself, your family and your assets; and earn untraceable income. *1996, 5½ x 8½, 138 pp, soft cover.* **$15.00.**

☐ **25065 ARMED DEFENSE, Gunfight Survival for the Householder and Businessman, by Burt Rapp.** This book is for the person who has decided to use a gun for protection. If you feel that extra locks and alarms are all you need for protection, then don't bother buying this book. But if you want to teach yourself to shoot well enough to save your life in a variety of ugly situations, this book is for you. You will learn techniques and tactics that work, not just reflections of somebody's theories. This book also covers what you need to know about the legal and emotional aspects of surviving a gunfight. *1989, 5½ x 8½, 214 pp, illustrated, soft cover.* **$16.95.**

☐ **55126 PRIVATE INVESTIGATION STRATEGIES AND TECHNIQUES, *by Angela Woodhull.*** Author Angela Woodhull is a private investigator with attitude. In this book, she tells us of her exploits ferreting out the truth for her clients and we are taken with her on some really wild excursions towards this end. Each case history is then analyzed to determine the strategies that made it work. While we may be entertained by her stories, we also learn successful methods to use ourselves, whether to find out information that involves you or someone you know, or if you are a private investigator with clients of your own. *2001, 5½ x 8½, 192 pp, soft cover.* $15.95.

☐ **25052 HOMEMADE GUNS AND HOMEMADE AMMO, *by Ronald B. Brown.*** How many "homemade gun" books have you read, only to discover that you need a metal lathe or milling machine? This book will teach you to make guns — and ammunition — with simple hand tools and everyday materials. Also covered are legalities, and concepts of ballistics. Step-by-step photographs, drawings, and plans show how to make: a 12-gauge shotgun; a muzzleloader; a double barrel; a wood gun; and much more. Five simple gunpowder recipes and two simple primer recipes are also included. *1986, 5½ 8½, 190 pp, illustrated, soft cover.* $14.95.

☐ **94281 101 THINGS TO DO 'TIL THE REVOLUTION, Ideas and resources for self-liberation, monkey wrenching and preparedness, *by Claire Wolfe.*** We don't need a weatherman to know which way the wind blows — but we do need the likes of Claire Wolfe, whose book offers 101 suggestions to help grease the wheels as we roll towards the government's inevitable collapse. Wolfe's list is lengthy and thought-provoking, as she elaborates on each piece of advice, from generalities to precise instructions. For the concerned citizen who wishes to keep a low profile, protect his or her rights, and survive in the "interesting times" which are sure to come, this is essential reading. *1996, 5½ x 8½, 216 pp, soft cover.* $15.95.